General editor: Graham Handley MA Ph.D.

Brodie's Notes on William Shakespeare's

Hamlet

Peter Washington MA M.Litt.
Senior Lecturer in Literary Studies, Middlesex Polyte

GW00726859

Pan Books London, Sydney and Auckland

References in these Notes are to the Arden Shakespeare: *Hamlet*, but as references are given to particular acts and scenes, the Notes may be used with any edition of the play.

First published 1991 by
Pan Books Ltd, Cavaye Place, London SW10 9PG

9 8 7 6 5 4 3 2 1

© Pan Books Ltd 1991

ISBN 0 330 50280 8

Photoset by Parker Typesetting Service, Leicester

Printed in England by Clays Ltd, St Ives plc

Contents

Preface by the general editor

This student revision aid is based on the principle that in any close examination of Shakespeare's plays 'the text's the thing'. Seeing a performance, or listening to a tape or record of a performance, is essential and is in itself a valuable and stimulating experience in understanding and appreciation. However, a real evaluation of Shakespeare's greatness, of his universality and of the nature of his literary and dramatic art, can only be achieved by constant application to the texts of the plays themselves. These revised editions of Brodie's Notes are intended to supplement that process through detailed critical commentary.

The first aim of each book is to fix the whole play in the reader's mind by providing a concise summary of the plot, relating it back, where appropriate, to its source or sources. Subsequently the book provides a summary of each scene, followed by *critical comments*. These may convey its importance in the dramatic structure of the play, creation of atmosphere, indication of character development, significance of figurative language etc, and they will also explain or paraphrase difficult words or phrases and identify meaningful references. At the end of each act revision questions are set to test the student's specific and broad understanding and appreciation of the play.

An extended critical commentary follows this scene by scene analysis. This embraces such major elements as characterization, imagery, the use of blank verse and prose, soliloquies and other aspects of the play which the editor considers need close attention. The paramount aim is to send the reader back to the text. The book concludes with a series of revision questions which require a detailed knowledge of the play; the first of these has notes by the editor of what *might* be included in a written answer. The intention is to stimulate and to guide; the whole emphasis of this commentary is to encourage the student's *involvement* in the play, to develop disciplined critical responses and thus promote personal enrichment through the imaginative experience of our greatest writer.

Graham Handley 1991

Shakespeare and the Elizabethan playhouse

William Shakespeare was born in Stratford-upon-Avon in 1564, and there are reasons to suppose that he came from a relatively prosperous family. He was probably educated at Stratford Grammar School and, at the age of eighteen, married Anne Hathaway, who was twenty-six. They had three children, a girl born shortly after their marriage, followed by twins in 1585 (the boy died in 1596). It seems likely that Shakespeare left for London shortly after a company of visiting players had visited Stratford in 1585, for by 1592 – according to the jealous testimony of one of his fellow-writers Robert Greene – he was certainly making his way both as actor and dramatist. The theatres were closed because of the plague in 1593; when they reopened Shakespeare worked with the Lord Chamberlain's Men, later the King's Men, and became a shareholder in each of the two theatres with which he was most closely associated, the Globe and the Blackfriars. He later purchased New Place, a considerable property in his home town of Stratford, to which he retired in 1611; there he entertained his great contemporary Ben Jonson (1572–1637) and the poet Michael Drayton (1563–1631). An astute businessman, Shakespeare lived comfortably in the town until his death in 1616.

This is a very brief outline of the life of our greatest writer, for little more can be said of him with certainty, though the plays – and poems – are living witness to the wisdom, humanity and many-faceted nature of the man. He was both popular and successful as a dramatist, perhaps less so as an actor. He probably began work as a dramatist in the late 1580s, by collaborating with other playwrights and adapting old plays, and by 1598 Francis Meres was paying tribute to his excellence in both comedy and tragedy. His first original play was probably *Love's Labour's Lost* (1590) and while the theatres were closed during the plague he wrote his narrative poems *Venus and Adonis* (1593) and *The Rape of Lucrece* (1594). The sonnets were almost certainly written in the 1590s, though not published until 1609; the first 126 seem to be addressed to a young man who was probably his friend and patron, while the rest are concerned with the 'dark lady'.

The dating of Shakespeare's plays has exercised scholars ever since the publication of the First Folio (1623), which listed them as comedies, histories and tragedies. It seems more important to look at them chronologically as far as possible, in order to trace Shakespeare's considerable development as a dramatist. The first period, say to the middle of the 1590s, included such plays as *Love's Labour's Lost*, *The Comedy of Errors*, *Richard III*, *The Taming of the Shrew*, *Romeo and Juliet* and *Richard II*. These early plays embrace the categories listed in the First Folio, so that Shakespeare the craftsman is evident in his capacity for variety of subject and treatment. The next phase includes *A Midsummer Night's Dream*, *The Merchant of Venice*, *Henry IV Parts 1 and 2*, *Henry V* and *Much Ado About Nothing*, as well as *Julius Caesar*, *As You Like It* and *Twelfth Night*. These are followed, in the early years of the seventeenth century, by his great tragic period: *Hamlet*, *Othello*, *King Lear* and *Macbeth*, with *Antony and Cleopatra* and *Coriolanus* belonging to 1607–09. The final phase embraces the romances (1610–13), *Cymbeline*, *The Tempest* and *The Winter's Tale* and the historical play *Henry VIII*.

Each of these revision aids will place the individual text under examination in the chronology of the remarkable dramatic output that spanned twenty years from the early 1590s to about 1613. The practical theatre for which Shakespeare wrote and acted derived from the inn courtyards in which performances had taken place, the few playhouses in his day being modelled on their structure. They were circular or hexagonal in shape, allowing the balconies and boxes around the walls full view of the stage. This large stage, which had no scenery, jutted out into the pit, the most extensive part of the theatre, where the poorer people – the 'groundlings' – stood. There was no roof (though the Blackfriars, used from 1608 onwards, was an indoor theatre) and thus bad weather meant no performance. Certain plays were acted at court, and these private performances normally marked some special occasion. Costumes, often rich ones, were used, and music was a common feature, with musicians on or under the stage; this sometimes had additional features, for example a trapdoor to facilitate the entry of a ghost. Women were barred by law from appearing on stage, and all female parts were played by boy actors; this undoubtedly explains the many instances in Shakespeare where a woman has to conceal her identity by disguising

herself as a man, e.g. Rosalind in *As You Like It*, Viola in *Twelfth Night*.

Shakespeare and his contemporaries often adapted their plays from sources in history and literature, extending an incident or a myth or creating a dramatic narrative from known facts. They were always aware of their own audiences, and frequently included topical references, sometimes of a satirical flavour, which would appeal to – and be understood by – the groundlings as well as their wealthier patrons who occupied the boxes. Shakespeare obviously learned much from his fellow dramatists and actors, being on good terms with many of them. Ben Jonson paid generous tribute to him in the lines prefaced to the First Folio of Shakespeare's plays:

Thou art a monument without a tomb,
And art alive still, while thy book doth live
And we have wits to read, and praise to give.

Among his contemporaries were Thomas Kyd (1558–94) and Christopher Marlowe (1564–93). Kyd wrote *The Spanish Tragedy*, the revenge motif here foreshadowing the much more sophisticated treatment evident in *Hamlet*, while Marlowe evolved the 'mighty line' of blank verse, a combination of natural speech and elevated poetry. The quality and variety of Shakespeare's blank verse owes something to the innovatory brilliance of Marlowe, but carries the stamp of individuality, richness of association, technical virtuosity and, above all, the genius of imaginative power.

The texts of Shakespeare's plays are still rich sources for scholars, and the editors of these revision aids have used the Arden editions of Shakespeare, which are regarded as pre-eminent for their scholarly approach. They are strongly recommended for advanced students, but other editions, like The New Penguin Shakespeare, The New Swan, and The Signet are all good annotated editions currently available. A reading list of selected reliable works on the play being studied is provided at the end of each commentary and students are advised to turn to these as their interest in the play deepens.

Literary terms used in these Notes

Alliteration Repetition of a consonant through several words, e.g. 'And I do doubt the hatch and the disclose/Will be some danger.'

Antithesis Contrasting words which express contrasting ideas, e.g. 'My words fly up, my thoughts remain below.'

Irony Expressing meaning by saying the opposite; it is often done unconsciously, e.g. 'And the King's rouse the heaven shall bruit again/Re-speaking earthly thunder' (Claudius is unknowingly fore-telling his own doom).

Dramatic irony The effectiveness of a scene depends partly upon a character's words and actions being the opposite of what is in fact happening, e.g. in III,1 Claudius agrees 'with all my heart,/It doth much content me' to watch the Players' performance without realizing that it has been set up to expose his guilt.

Image One object or idea used to express another, e.g. 'Virtue itself scapes not calumnious strokes./The canker galls the infants of the spring.'

Metaphor Expressing one thing directly in terms of another, without using 'as' or 'like', e.g. 'How weary, stale, flat and unprofitable/Seem to me all the uses of this world!/Fie on't, ah fie, 'tis an unweeded garden.'

Oxymoron The combination of contradictory terms, e.g. bitter-sweet.

Personification Addressing an object as if it were a person, e.g. 'But look, the morn in russet mantle clad/Walks o'er the dew of yon high eastward hill.'

Pun Playing with two or more meanings of a single word, e.g. in I,2 'son' used by Claudius, picked up as 'sun' by Hamlet.

Simile Explaining one thing in terms of another using the words 'as' or 'like', e.g. 'Now see that noble and most sovereign reason/Like sweet bells jangled out of tune and harsh.'

Symbol Using one thing to stand for another or for a series of things, e.g. the Ghost, 'Be thou a spirit of health/Or goblin damned.'

The play

Plot

The plot of Shakespeare's longest play can be summed up in one brief phrase: Hamlet avenges his father's murder. But while the succinctness of this formula tells us a lot about what holds a rambling drama together, it doesn't suggest the extraordinary richness and complexity of the play. To do that, we need a closer focus.

Thinking about *Hamlet* purely in terms of revenge, we might describe the plot like this: at the beginning of the play, Claudius, the murderer, has married his brother's widow and usurped the throne. Shortly afterwards, the ghost of the dead king reveals the truth to young Hamlet, who resolves to avenge his father. But for one reason or another, Hamlet delays his revenge. Meanwhile Claudius, counselled by Polonius, strikes first, sending Hamlet off to be murdered in England.

When Hamlet foils the plot and returns to Denmark, Claudius decides to try again. He encourages Polonius's son Laertes to challenge Hamlet to a duel in which Laertes will have a sharpened, poisoned rapier and Hamlet a harmless blunt one. To make doubly sure Claudius also supplies a poisoned goblet for Hamlet to drink from. But although Hamlet is mortally wounded, the plan goes wrong. In their scuffle the duellists exchange rapiers, Laertes himself is wounded, and the Queen drinks from the poisoned goblet. When the dying Laertes reveals the King's stratagem, Hamlet kills Claudius with the poisoned rapier before dying himself.

This account of the plot focuses on the two opponents: Claudius the murderer and Hamlet his avenging nephew. But in doing so, it omits all the elements which raise *Hamlet* above the common run of revenge tragedies in Shakespeare's time. It says nothing about Hamlet's relationship with his parents, his feelings for Ophelia, or – most important of all – his own complex emotional, moral and spiritual condition. It might be said that none of these things is essential to the plot: Hamlet could decide to avenge his father whatever the state of his mind or relationships, simply because of the aristocratic code which demanded such behaviour. But as we shall see, much critical discussion of the play rages around just this point: how far are Hamlet's personal circumstances there to provide motivation for the revenge plot, and how far is the plot simply a peg on which to hang a study of Hamlet the character?

We can see some of the issues involved here if we provide a more elaborate description of the action, taking into account Hamlet's situation and state of mind, in order to show how these affect the action of the play.

When the play opens, he is disturbed and disgusted by his mother's hasty remarriage, even before he knows the truth about his father's death. It is this disgust, combined with horror at the Ghost's revelations, which prompts the furious interview with Queen Gertrude during which the concealed Polonius is killed, thus prompting Laertes to seek his own revenge and helping to precipitate the final catastrophe. Furthermore, Polonius's presence in Getrude's room is dictated in part by concern for his own daughter, Ophelia, to whom Hamlet has been making advances.

But by this time, Claudius realizes that Hamlet knows the truth, and so uses Polonius's death as an excuse to bring forward Hamlet's proposed diplomatic mission to England, where he is to be killed by Claudius's allies. Meanwhile, Hamlet has been feigning madness (the 'antic disposition') to fool his enemies into attributing his behaviour to the wrong cause and to put them off their guard. Her father's death, combined with Hamlet's cruelty, however, push Ophelia into the real madness which brings about her death. The demise of both his father and sister, apparently at Hamlet's hands, prompts the hot-headed Laertes to enter into a conspiracy with Claudius to dispose of the prince by fighting a 'fixed' duel with him when he returns unexpectedly from his trip after the encounter with pirates.

On his return Hamlet seems to be changed: chastened and fatalistic. He no longer feigns madness, or devises elaborate schemes such as the Dumbshow to trap Claudius, but resolves to take events as they come. By this time, however, 'events' have their own momentum, and even his reconciliation with Laertes, the instrument of Claudius's will, is not enough to prevent the final catastrophe which sweeps away the ruling family.

Sources

It seems probable that *Hamlet* owes something to a contemporary version of the same subject, but this play is lost. There were, however, other sources available to Shakespeare which throw light on his treatment of the drama.

The recognizable story of Hamlet (known as Amleth) first appears in the Historiae Danicae, published in 1514 but written at the end of the twelfth century by the historian Saxo. The text foreshadows the main outlines of the plot – fratricide, incest, assumed madness, and revenge – and several of the characters are recognizable, but it is highly unlikely that Shakespeare knew this account, and he probably found his material from the version of the story in Belleforest's *Histoires Tragiques*, or from a translation of the French original.

In Saxo, Amleth is given various adventures, surviving the death of his uncle to become king. The episode borrowed by Shakespeare via Belleforest contains most of *Hamlet*'s major features, with the significant exception of the Ghost. Amleth's feigned madness is explained by the need to protect himself from his uncle by pretending to be half-witted (and therefore no threat). A girl who was his childhood companion is set to seduce him so that he will reveal to her his real state of mind, but she takes his side, as does his foster brother – clearly the originals of Ophelia and Horatio. One of the new king's advisers is killed when spying on Amleth in conversation with his mother. Amleth is then sent to England to be killed, but returns in secret while his own funeral is being conducted, later surprising and killing his sleeping uncle.

Belleforest makes few changes to the plot in his version of the story, but he expands it to include high-flown speeches and moralizing comment, foreshadowing the great set pieces of Shakespeare's play. Hints of the supernatural are introduced, and the theme of just revenge is underlined. Whereas in Saxo we are invited to admire the cunning way in which the hero outwits his enemies, Belleforest emphasizes Amleth's nobility.

Shakespeare's re-working of this material, which may owe something to the lost earlier version of *Hamlet*, throws considerable light on the play. We can see this if we consider the major changes he made.

First there is the Ghost. Though the spirits of the underworld are referred to in Belleforest, the Ghost is clearly a major addition to the plot mechanism, providing Hamlet with his motive and his justification for killing Claudius. This was not a new idea. Visitors from the underworld became a popular way of stimulating theatrical nerves, and there was the example of Seneca, a Roman tragedian whose work had a profound influence on sixteenth-century drama, and who uses the trick several times. Even more familiar to Shakespeare would be *The Spanish Tragedy* by Kyd, possibly author of the first *Hamlet*.

Shakespeare's second important modification to the original material is the idea of the two families: Hamlet/Gertrude/Claudius/Old Hamlet, and Polonius/Laertes/Ophelia. This, like the invention of the Ghost, helps to pull the somewhat diffuse original story together, focusing our attention on the similarities and differences between the two families, and introducing a whole chain of ironies lacking in Belleforest and Saxo.

The third improvement on the originals comes from the playwright's concentration on a single situation and theme: revenge for the death of a father. Though *Hamlet* is a long, complicated play, it is immeasurably more forceful than the sources.

A fourth change involves the introduction of the Players. While most of Shakespeare's alterations work in the interest of dramatic economy, this clearly goes the other way, adding a major new element to the play and helping to lengthen it. The idea for the Dumbshow and 'The Murder of Gonzago' may very well be taken from *The Spanish Tragedy*, in which a father avenges his son's death by means of staging a play within the play, but Shakespeare typically goes much further than Kyd by working the imagery of performance into his text. In my view, this fourth change is the most characteristic and the most important, because it completely changes the significance of the story. What might remain a bloody, moral tale takes on the complex philosophical overtones which have fascinated audiences to this day (for more on this point see the sections on Themes and Style on pages 78–92).

Scene summaries, critical commentary, textual notes and revision questions

Act I Scene 1

Nominally the changing of the guard on the castle battlements, the action in this strange scene is minimal. Barnardo relieves Francisco on guard; Horatio and Marcellus arrive to watch for the Ghost; the Ghost appears. The watchers discuss the meaning of the apparition; it comes back; dawn breaks and the apparition vanishes. The scene is really more concerned with atmosphere than with action, which it refers to only obliquely. What matters is the sense of unease and anticipation, as in the overture to an opera which hints at themes and establishes the prevailing mood. So the complicated (and rather tedious) explanation of the rivalry between Norway and Denmark, which appears to be setting up the plot, turns out to be more important as another sign of the disorder portended by the appearance of the Ghost.

The action is both mundane and bizarre. Perhaps this combination of the ordinary and the peculiar is what makes the scene so unsettling. It certainly affects the style, which ranges from the colloquial opening exchanges, through Horatio's formal narrative, to the quiet, radiant lyricism of the ending.

The scene makes an emotional progress from dread to relief, from darkness to light, from night to day, which foreshadows the movement of the whole play from the dark corruption of Claudius's Denmark to the hope signalled by Fortinbras.

Commentary

unfold Explain. Observe how the play begins on a mysterious note. Both sentinels are nervous and challenge each other.

carefully . . . hour Punctually.

sick at heart This is not explained, but it contributes to the general sense of unease, foreshadowing the 'sickness' of both Hamlet and the state.

rivals Partners.

the Dane The king of Denmark.

Give you . . . May God grant you.

is Horatio there Once again there is a moment of uncertainty.

A piece of him i.e., his hand. But this may also hint that Horatio's heart is not in his task, or that he remains sceptical. See l.27 below.

Touching Concerning.

of By.

along To come along.

approve our eyes Confirm what we have seen.

speak to it Ghosts traditionally speak only to the person for whom they have a message. Hence the later refusal to speak to anyone but Hamlet.

assail ... fortified ... Taking a metaphor from their presence on the castle battlements, Barnardo says he will attempt to persuade the sceptical Horatio that they really have seen the Ghost.

Last night of all As recently as last night.

illume Illuminate.

beating Sounding. Shakespeare brings in the Ghost on cue, saving Barnardo (and us) the trouble of his narrative.

In the same figure like With a similar appearance to ... It isn't yet certain that this is the king's ghost.

scholar ... There are two points here: (i) spirits were exorcized in Latin, the language of the church; (ii) As an intellectual, Horatio is better suited to the task than simple soldiers.

a He.

usurp'st Takes possession of.

majesty ... Denmark King of Denmark. A complicated play on words in which 'buried' is transferred from 'majesty' to 'Denmark'.

Did sometimes Used to.

Stay, speak See above l.32.

sensible and true avouch Evidence. Sensible means 'made aware through the senses'. The sceptical Horatio takes nothing on trust – which makes the reality of the Ghost all the more convincing.

Norway The King of Norway, father to Fortinbras. Notice how this prepares the way for Horatio's narrative.

parle Encounter.

sledded Polacks Poles in sledges.

'Tis strange Horatio is still doubtful. He can't yet decide that this really is the dead king.

jump Precisely. Such repeated precision suggests the Ghost's urgent sense of purpose.

martial stalk Military tread. Observe how Old Hamlet's fierce and soldierly character is constantly emphasized.

In what ... know not I don't understand how to make exact sense of this.

the gross ... opinion In general terms.

bodes ... eruption Portends some violent disturbance. A common explanation of unusual events, e.g. comets.

Good, now ... As if to say, 'Having got that much clear...' Marcellus then seems to change gear abruptly, moving from the Ghost to the disturbed state of Denmark, asking why it is that they must keep such vigilant watch. As Horatio's speech makes clear, this transition is suggested by the apparition's armour, which recalls old conflicts now flaring up. But the exchange turns out to be ironic, for the violent eruption in the state will be the result, not of the old king's wars but of his murder.

toils the subject Makes the people work – much as the Ghost is made to 'work'. The sense of tension is general.

why Why is there . . .

cast Casting. Note the opposition of 'nightly' (for the sentries) and 'daily' for the others, taken up in 'make the night joint-labourer with the day'.

mart Trade.

impress Forced labour.

What might be toward What is about to happen.

Who is't . . . Compare l.73 for Marcellus's insistence on asking someone who knows, i.e. Horatio.

whisper Rumour.

prick'd on Urged on.

emulate Jealous. Refers to Fortinbras.

our valiant Hamlet . . . i.e. Prince Hamlet's father, Old Hamlet.

this side of our known world This probably means Europe.

seal'd compact Formal agreement. The two kings fought according to carefully stated rules.

moiety competent Equal portion. Each king staked the same amount of land.

gaged Offered as a pledge.

which had . . . vanquisher Which would have become the property of Fortinbras, had he won. The very stately language here is suitable to the chivalric theme of personal combat between kings. Whether this long-winded speech is appropriate in this scene, is another matter. However, it serves to establish Old Hamlet's princely, warlike character, later dwelt on by his son.

cov'nant Agreement.

carriage . . . design'd Meaning of the agreement.

unimproved mettle Untrained ardour.

skirts Outer regions.

Shark'd up a list Gathered a gang. 'Shark'd' suggests both urgency and roughness.

lawless resolutes Ruffians.

For food and diet to To use in.

That hath a stomach in't Which requires daring. The play on words here depends on the traditional view of the stomach as the source of courage (and cowardice).

which is . . . lost Which is, from our point of view, nothing but an attempt to take from us by force the lands his father lost.

compulsatory Imposed.

the main motive Fortinbras's attempt to avenge his father's death anticipates Hamlet's attempt to do the same. They both succeed.

head Origin, as of a stream or fountain.

sort Suit.

portentous Foreshadowing. Horatio elaborates this idea in the following speech.

through During.

was and is Notice here the constant linking of past and present.

the question Cause.

palmy state Thriving condition. This description is traditional.

Julius Julius Caesar. The mightiest because the greatest of the Caesars.

As stars . . . fire Comets (see l.72 above). The syntax is awkward here. There seems to be a verb missing.

the moist star The moon. The moon moves the tides, hence 'Neptune's empire'.

Upon Under.

And even . . . countrymen This absurdly over-written sentence in Shakespeare's worst vein simply means that the Ghost is to Denmark as the portents of Caesar's death were to the Romans, which seems to hint at Claudius's downfall.

And . . . precurse And so the similar anticipation.

omen Event.

climatures Country, or climes.

soft Peace.

cross Confront.

privy Familiar.

partisan Spear.

majestical . . . as the air . . . Marcellus gives two quite different reasons for not striking the Ghost.

malicious mockery i.e. only the mockery of real blows.

fearful Both the Ghost and the summons are fearful.

extravagant Straying.

herein i.e. the truth of what Horatio has heard.

probation Proof.

Some say . . . Notice that Horatio and Marcellus both report speech, a neat way for Shakespeare to avoid giving credence to pagan beliefs.

bird of dawning Cock.

strike Blight. Like the reference to the stars in Horatio's earlier speech, this evokes astrology.

in part Horatio's characteristic scepticism.

Act I Scene 2

Claudius regrets his brother's death but celebrates his own marriage to that brother's widow. He dismisses Fortinbras's threat and sends greetings to the king of Norway (Fortinbras's uncle). He gives Laertes, son of Polonius, permission to return to Paris, but urges Hamlet not to go back to Wittenberg. The King and Queen then leave Hamlet alone after begging him not to indulge his grief, and in his first soliloquy the prince reflects on his own despair and his mother's remarriage. The scene ends when Horatio enters to announce the appearance of the Ghost and Hamlet vows to watch for it that night.

In sharp contrast with the cold, dramatic exterior of the castle dominated by his dead brother, we move in this scene to the formal setting of the new court where Claudius, surrounded by family, advisers and courtiers, attempts to put aside the period of mourning in order to establish his own personality and policy. We see him acting in a thoroughly statesmanlike and magnanimous way, and at this stage of the proceedings, his urbanity contrasts not unfavourably with Hamlet's brusque rudeness. Yet we already know from l.1 that this easy-going manner covers considerable political and military turmoil. Taken together, these circumstances point to the difference between Hamlet's sincerity and Claudius's duplicity – a difference fundamental to the play.

The King's first speech is formal and dignified – its fluency contrasting ironically with his dead brother's anguished silence. But Hamlet, it might be said, has no ears for what Claudius has to say, and his own long, impassioned soliloquy half-way through the scene shows why. Listening to Hamlet we understand the shallowness of Claudius's formal regret for his brother's death, and our sympathy swings round towards his nephew. This is the first of many changes of standpoint in the play which cause us constantly to revise our estimate of the major characters.

The other characters – even the Queen – are all grouped round this central contrast which has not yet become an open conflict. And despite the formal setting, the focus of the scene is personal. There is no sense that Hamlet resents his uncle politically. However inadequate the King's feelings may be, his rights are not in question – a point underlined by Hamlet's concentration on his mother's failings in the soliloquy at l.129. But as Hamlet's sombre clothing shows, he is isolated: at this stage in the action, he is very much the odd one out, apart from the court and his family. In consequence, we notice his marked change in tone when Horatio enters, and grief and bitterness turn to warmth. Yet the end of the scene changes the mood again, when discussion of the Ghost returns us to the uneasiness of I,1.

Commentary

dear brother Under the laws of Denmark, Claudius has every right to the throne, which was elective. As we soon discover, he is unsuited by character, not by law.

that it us befitted Though it is right for us.

contracted ... woe Joined in sorrow. But notice the play on the royal 'we' which lets Claudius link his courtiers with his own feelings.

Yet so far ... The following lines – and Claudius's words to Hamlet – indicate a careful balancing of feeling ('nature') against practicality ('discretion'), 'him' against 'ourselves' (in which term Claudius again includes everyone).

jointress Joint-ruler. But this is true in name only.

defeated joy A virtual oxymoron which leads to a whole series of oppositions in the following lines: auspicious/dropping, mirth/dirge, delight/dole. These reinforce the sense of careful balance mentioned above. Claudius is speaking for public consumption.

auspicious ... dropping Smiling ... weeping.

dole Grief.

barr'd Ignored.

better ... along The specific sense is unclear here. The general sense is that the courtiers approve (or appear to) Claudius's marriage and his brief period of mourning for the late king.

Now follows The next point is.

weak supposal Poor opinion.

disjoint ... frame Disordered.

Colleagued Allied.

Importing Requesting.

gait Proceeding in this matter.

full proportions Necessary numbers.

subject People. The point here is that when Old Norway hears that Fortinbras has been levying troops from the Norwegians, he will put a stop to it.

To business For business.

dilated Extensive.

commend Proclaim or express.

And now, Laertes ... Notice that the King turns first to the war, then to Laertes, and last of all to Hamlet. This gives the audience time to watch the Prince brooding on stage, and prepares the way for him to dominate the second part of the scene. It also suggests Claudius's care not to pay him too much attention.

lose your voice Waste your breath.

my offer ... asking Offered by me even before you ask for it.

native Related.

instrumental Necessary. The organic metaphor, comparing the parts of the state to the parts of the body, is common in Shakespeare.

slow Reluctant.

Upon ... consent To his desire I gave my firm agreement.

Take ... hour Enjoy your youth.

graces Qualities. This eulogy on Laertes invites us to compare him favourably with the gloomy Hamlet.

cousin ... son ... Cousin is the common term of address between royal relations, but Hamlet is also a kind of son to Claudius. In the next line Hamlet denies this closeness.

A ... kind Close in blood relationship but lacking natural affinity.

clouds May refer to Hamlet's dark mood and also his dark clothes.

in the sun ... The pun with 'son' here refers back to the previous lines. Hamlet is in an odd situation, with three parents – but one is dead, one he resents, and the third (his mother) he has mixed feelings about.

nighted Black. How appropriate that Hamlet should wear the colour of the time when the Ghost appears.

vailed Lowered.

in the dust Dramatic irony. Old Hamlet is up and about!

common ... There is irony here, too. Although death is common, murder and haunting are not.

Seems ... This is the first of Hamlet's reflections on appearance and reality, a common theme in this play and Shakespearian tragedy in general. Hamlet claims that his grief is more than show – hinting at the difference between him and Claudius in l.84.

windy ... breath Deep sighing.

dejected ... visage Downcast look.

duties ... Claudius rejects Hamlet's claim.

To ... sorrow To perform the appropriate rites.

But to ... Claudius finds various arguments against Hamlet's behaviour. He stresses that it is contrary to both nature and divine law – thus implying their sanction for his own position.

incorrect Undisciplined.

As ... sense As anything we know.

peevish Perverse.

throw to earth ... i.e. bury with your father.

unprevailing Pointless.

the most immediate The next in succession. Claudius seeks to reassure Hamlet here.

impart Feel and display.

retrograde . . . desire Against our will. It isn't clear how far Claudius says this simply because he wants Hamlet where he can see him.

our eye See ll.11 and 69. The emphasis with Claudius is constantly on appearance.

in . . . best As well as I can. Hamlet addresses his mother and ignores Claudius.

Be as ourself Have the same rights and pleasures. The words are ironic.

Sits . . . heart Pleases me.

grace Thanks.

rouse Drinking.

bruit Noise abroad.

Re-speaking Notice how the King speaks of himself as linking earth and heaven again – and see comment on l.92. By emphasizing his own semi-divine role, Claudius strengthens his legitimacy and authority.

O that this . . . Hamlet's first major soliloquy, in which he explains his state of mind. For detailed comment, see the section on Hamlet's character. But note the contrast between the broken, emotional style of this speech, and the smoothness of what goes before.

sullied There has been intense critical debate about 'sullied'. The textual evidence for this word is confused. Some editors accept 'sullied', meaning contamined. Others think the word should be solid; and yet others plump for 'sallied', meaning assailed. It is up to the reader to determine the sense from context, here and elsewhere.

canon Law, i.e. the sixth commandment.

unweeded garden A common image in this play and elsewhere in sixteenth-century literature.

merely Entirely. The generality of Hamlet's disgust is focused in the following comments on his mother.

Hyperion to a satyr The sun-god compared with a goat-man. This comparison opens a long sequence of references through the play to the double nature of Man (part god, part beast). Here bestiality has got the upper hand in both Claudius and Gertrude.

beteem Allow.

Heaven and earth . . . See notes to ll.92 and 127. Notice also the reiterated distinction: god/beast, heaven/earth, Old Hamlet/Claudius.

hang Dote.

or ere Before.

Niobe The personification of maternal sorrow in Greek mythology.

a beast . . . See l.140 above. Also III,4. In Renaissance thought, Man is characterized as the creature with reason – below the angels, above the beasts.

unrighteous False (because her grief is contradicted by her behaviour).

flushing . . . galled eyes Redness in her sore eyes.

post Haste.

incestuous . . . Because she has married her husband's brother.

that name . . . i.e. servant.

And . . . from And what are you doing away from . . .

drink deep . . . Drinking plays a large part at the Danish court. The Danes were notorious for drunkenness in Shakespeare's time.

funeral . . . wedding . . . An ironic reference to Claudius's first speech. Hamlet is obsessed.

I see . . . Anticipating Horatio's news. The old king's appearance plays an important part, both as Ghost and as the remembered fine figure of a man. See also below l.187.

a man . . . Quite. Neither a beast nor the god Hamlet invoked earlier.

I shall not . . . But of course, that's just what he will do. There is a further irony here, because it is not quite his father he sees.

Season your admiration Moderate your astonishment.

attent Attentive.

deliver/Upon Explain with.

at point exactly, cap-à-pie Perfect in every detail from top to toe.

Appears Note the change to the present tense, increasing the sense of immediacy.

Within . . . length The distance of his staff.

distill'd Dissolved.

act Effect.

like Like one another.

even then At that moment.

beaver Faceguard.

What How.

warn't Warrant, i.e. believe.

And . . . tongue And whatever else may happen tonight, think about it but say nothing.

requite Reward.

Foul deeds . . . It is common to end a scene with a rhyming couplet, especially when a general principle is being stated, as here. The notion that crimes cannot be hidden, that the truth will always out, is common in Shakespeare and elsewhere.

Act I Scene 3

Laertes warns Ophelia not to pay attention to Hamlet's wooing. It is then his turn to receive advice from Polonius before leaving for Paris. The two speeches are worth comparing. After that, Polonius repeats Laertes' warning to Ophelia and orders her to spend no more time with Hamlet.

Another change of scene, but this time to the other family in the play, emphasizing the parallels between the two. The relationship between parents and children is a constant theme, with Polonius, Claudius, Getrude, Old Hamlet and Old Norway on the one hand; Laertes, Ophelia, Hamlet and Fortinbras on the other. But the grandeur and melancholy of the previous scene are here replaced by the ordinary, and even the comic: Laertes' bossiness with his sister, his impatience to leave, and Polonius's tedious advice. But the undercurrent of the tragedy is still there in the shape of Hamlet, always present in name and influence if not in body. It might be said that he haunts this family much as the Ghost haunts his.

Commentary

convoy is assistant means of transport are available.

For Hamlet . . . This complicated paragraph points out that Hamlet's desires are urgent but transient, the careless pleasures of a prince.
  a toy in blood Passing fancy. Does Laertes speak from experience?
  primy In its prime.
  suppliance Occupation.

nature crescent Horatio offers a realistic assessment of Ophelia's situation. A prince is unlike other men in apparently contrary respects: i) he can indulge his whims at her expense, but ii) he must ultimately act in the best interest of the state – also possibly at her expense. The phrase 'nature crescent' suggests that as Hamlet develops he will lose interest in the girl. There is also a sense of 'nature' which suggests 'desire'. So the sense of the speech is that Hamlet may be pure in his intentions now, but neither his purity nor his interest in her are likely to survive the pressure (political and personal) which maturity will bring.

thews and bulk Strength and size.
  temple Body.

The inward . . . withal So do the mind and soul.

cautel Cunning.

virtue of his will Purity of his feeling (towards you).

His greatness weigh'd Taking his position into account.
  his will . . . Notice the play on 'will' which at one moment means sexual desire, at another freedom to act.

on his choice . . . This is one of the central ideas of the play, a commonplace of sixteenth-century thought: that the health of the state depends directly on the wisdom and moral probity of the ruler. Hence the later reflections on Claudius.

body ... head See l.20 above.

his ... place His unique behaviour and situation.

give ... deed Suit his actions to his words.

main ... withal Danes will consent to.

credent Trusting.

chaste treasure Virginity.

in the rear Military metaphor in which Laertes advises his sister to be cautious.

chariest Most cautious.

scapes ... strokes Escapes not slanderous remarks.

galls Blights.

buttons Buds.

liquid Bright.

blastments Infections. Notice how Laertes refers back to the spring imagery of l.7.

best safety ... Compare Polonius's advice to his son.

Youth ... near Self-restraint is no check to the desires of youth, even though there is no one else to stir them.

recks not his own rede Does not follow his own advice. Ophelia stands up for herself – and hints that Laertes isn't above approach. See note on l.6 above.

O fear me not This seems to mean 'Don't worry', i.e. I will take my own advice.

Occasion ... upon A fortunate chance for.

leave Leave-taking. Somewhat ironic in view of the unwanted advice Polonius now hands out.

The wind ... sail Your boat is ready to leave.

character Write.

Give ... act Hold your tongue and don't act on impulse.

their adoption tried Their friendship tested.

dull thy palm Waste your money.

courage Buck or dandy.

Bear't that Deport yourself so that.

voice Support.

censure Opinion.

fancy Ornament. Here Polonius seems to be advising Laertes to avoid all the things he (like most young men) wants to do.

in that i.e. in their dressing.

husbandry This can mean saving, economy or industry.

to thine ... true Be consistent.

season Ripen.

invests Presses. A military metaphor. To invest a fortress is to besiege it.

tend Attend.

Given . . . you Seen you in private.

free Generous.

put on Urged on – presumably by Gertrude and Claudius.

tenders Expressions.

green Inexperienced. A continuation of the spring metaphors.

Unsifted Inexperienced.

Tender Offer. The commercial metaphor continues, but there is also a play on the other sense in which 'tender' means take more care of yourself. The link between financial and amorous affairs is ominous. It also points to the duplicity of the scene in which Ophelia is instructed to pretend to return Hamlet's affection as part of her father's 'payment' to Claudius.

crack the wind Metaphor taken from horses meaning 'overstrain' – which is of course just what Polonius typically does with his over-elaborate play on words in the next phrase.

tender me a fool A further pun. The phrase can mean 'Make a fool of me' and 'Offer me a fool', i.e. Ophelia herself.

importun'd Pressed.

fashion This recalls l.6. Polonius persists in turning Ophelia's words to his own sense, just as he uses her for his own purpose later.

countenance Confirmation.

springes Snares.

When the blood burns . . . Polonius takes up his son's warning. Fire is a common image for sexual desire.

   prodigal Generously. Desire prompts men to deceptive eloquence.

more light than heat More show than substance.

   extinct . . . The sense here depends upon the paradox that fire consumes its own source in order to exist. In the very moment the passionate man speaks, the passion which impelled him to speak is fading.

scanter More sparing.

entreatments Negotiations. Once again Polonius revives the commercial metaphor.

so much in him This much of him.

a larger tether More freedom – because he is a man and also a prince. Polonius again echoes his son.

brokers Agents. Back to the commercial metaphor.

dye Colour. Again the distinction between appearance and reality.

   investments Clothes.

implorators Beseechers.

pious bawds This continues the reality/appearance dichotomy. It means brothel-keepers who pretend to virtue.

for all Final.

slander Abuse, i.e. waste.
Come your ways Be about your business. Colloquial.

Act I Scene 4

Hamlet, Horatio and Marcellus watch for the Ghost on the battlements. Hearing the sound of trumpets which accompanies the King's revels, Hamlet regrets the Danish reputation for drunkenness and reflects on the origins of human frailty. The Ghost appears and beckons Hamlet to follow. He does so, and his companions trail behind at a distance.

This scene returns us to the place and atmosphere of I,1, but with an ironic twist given by the distant sound of the King's revelry – ironic, because Claudius's downfall is about to begin as he celebrates his power and the Ghost appears to Hamlet.

Commentary

shrewdly Bitterly.
eager Sharp.
lacks of Is just before.
it is struck We return to both the place and the time of the play's beginning.
wake Stays awake, in order to celebrate.
wassail Revelry.
 reels Dances. The upspring is an energetic dance.
Rhenish German wine.
triumph ... pledge The news of his toast. But Hamlet speaks ironically, hence 'triumph'.
Is is a custom? Apparently it was. But see I,2,125.
to the manner born Hamlet is not only familiar with the custom; it is part of the society he belongs to (and somewhat dislikes).
traduc'd and tax'd of Exposed to contempt and condemned by.
clepe Call.
our addition The way they describe us.
The pith ... attribute The very core of our esteem. The idea here is that the reputation for drinking detracts from even their greatest achievements.
particular men Individuals (as opposed to whole nations).
mole Blemish.
As in ... guilty Inherited.
nature ... Notice the loose uses of this word which here means 'any part of nature', i.e. any individual man.

complexion This is the combination of the four humours (blood, choler, melancholy, phlegm) which were supposed to constitute human beings according to the Greek theory inherited by the Elizabethans. Here Shakespeare extends the word to mean one of those humours. Once the balance is destroyed, the individual may be damaged to the point of madness.

pales Defensive fences. More military metaphors.

o'erleavens Undermines.

plausive manners Acceptable behaviour.

livery Servants' uniform.

else Other.

undergo Sustain.

general censure Common opinion. Hamlet is referring here not to a man's character but his reputation. This interest in appearances seems to go against his insistence on the real self as opposed to show (see I,2,76), but we need to make a crucial distinction here between false appearances and rightful ones: it is the first sort Hamlet objects to. Like anyone else in his time he believes in the vital importance of the second sort. A man's honour depends on his reputation – on how others see him – and honour is an all-important motive. It is perhaps appropriate that the Ghost should appear at the end of this speech, because it is the Ghost who spurs Hamlet on to honourable revenge.

dout Extinguish.

To Resulting in.

spirit of health Good angel (bringing 'airs from heaven').

questionable Inviting questions. And the Ghost will answer only Hamlet's questions, no one else's.

in ignorance . . . i.e. with frustration.

canoniz'd Consecrated.

  hearsed Coffined.

cerements Shroud.

inurn'd Entombed.

complete steel Full armour.

fools of nature i.e. because this is an event beyond their understanding. Another use of the word 'nature'.

disposition Mind.

some impartment Something to impart.

to . . . ground Further away.

beetles o'er Overhangs.

Act I Scene 5

The Ghost tells Hamlet how he was killed and demands revenge, which Hamlet agrees to mete out to Claudius. Horatio and

Marcellus enter and Hamlet swears them to silence about what they have witnessed, and about the madness he intends to feign. Scene 5 completes the first part of the play's action and all the exposition. Apart from a brief appearance in Act III Scene 4 the Ghost does not appear again. Nor do Marcellus and Barnardo. All three have served their purpose. Hamlet has been shaken out of his depression by the shock of the encounter, which gives him a motive for action – and the comments on madness suggest that he has already begun to form a plan. The other main characters have been introduced, the past has been explained: it now remains for the action to grind inexorably on. From this point attention is on Hamlet: when will he achieve his revenge, and how will he do it?

Commentary

Mark me ... The Ghost speaks to Hamlet and to no one else. Later (in Act III, Scene 4), this causes Hamlet's mother to believe in his madness.

My hour ... Dawn.

days of nature Lifetime. Yet another use of 'nature'.

porpentine Porcupine.

eternal blazon Description of life after death.

apt Ready.

Lethe The river of forgetfulness in the Greek underworld.

ear People. Note the playful anticipation of l.63, which implies that Claudius has poisoned the people's minds with lies in the same way he poisoned the old king's body.

forged process Invented description.

prophetic Though Hamlet didn't suspect the murder, he instinctively mistrusted his uncle.

seeming-virtuous This phrase points to an important problem in the play. Though Gertrude has succumbed to Claudius, Shakespeare doesn't want to present her too unsympathetically. The solution is for the Ghost to condemn Gertrude while accepting that Claudius's wiles were too strong to resist. Hamlet is also instructed to spare his mother (l.86 below) though it may be that this is more to preserve the prince from the sin of matricide than to protect Gertrude, who is to be left to Heaven's justice and her own remorse. But the Ghost seems especially outraged by the fact that Gertrude could prefer a poor specimen like Claudius after the honour of being married to him. It is thus not only her lustfulness he objects to, and her choice of partner, but her betrayal of his own magnificence. This would be comic were it not that the Ghost is not so much a character as the enunciator of a certain view of life, and the source of Hamlet's motive.

the vow ... It is not clear whether the Ghost means one particular vow – to be faithful – or the general vows of marriage.

sate Indulge.

garbage i.e. Claudius.

secure hour Hour of relaxation.

hebenon Poison.

leperous Scale-making.

gates and alleys Just as the state may be compared to a body, so a body is compared to a town.

posset Thicken.

eager Sour.

tetter bark'd about Skin disease spread over.

lazar-like Leper-like.

Unhousel'd, disappointed, unanel'd Without receiving the Eucharist, unprepared and unanointed. All three terms refer to the practice of preparing individuals for death with the last rites of the church. These can only be administered after the confession of sins – the reckoning mentioned in the following line. Without such rites the dead cannot be accepted into Paradise without further penance.

sent to Sent to settle, i.e. with God.

nature Natural feeling (for his father).

luxury Lust. Notice how the Ghost constantly returns to this – as he regards it with more horror than his own murder. Yet in the following lines he orders Hamlet to spare his mother. This is more complex than a simple demand for revenge.

Taint not ... See note on l.46 above.

couple hell ... Hamlet thinks of invoking all the hosts, i.e. spirits of heaven, earth and hell. See I,2,142. As there, the invocation gives a sense of the cosmic scale of the action.

stiffly A pun here on 'stiff' meaning strong and 'stiff' meaning old.

globe Another pun on head/world.

fond Foolish.

saws Sayings.

pressures Impressions.

tables Notebooks.

Writes There is, of course, no need for Hamlet to write this down. So why does he do it? As a rhetorical flourish, a sort of contract with himself. At such an overwhelming moment of emotional stress he must *do* something.

my word My motto. Hamlet doesn't need to be told to remember his father either, but the Ghost has crystallized in the phrase 'remember me' what his son is already inclined to do. More important still, he has made this phrase a plan of action, not merely an emotional disposition.

secure Protect.

Hillo, ho, ho A hawking cry.

There's never . . . Hamlet makes a joke out of his news by stating the obvious. This is the beginning of a change of mood from melancholy to teasing. Having acquired a purpose – 'business and desire' as he says at l.136 – he intends to keep that purpose secret.

whirling Excited.

heartily . . . The repetitions, like the jokiness, underline Hamlet's exhilaration here. They also suggest his mercurial temperament.

O'ermaster't Control it.

not I Horatio isn't refusing to swear but agreeing to Hamlet's request.

truepenny Honest chap.

hic et ubique Here and everywhere (Latin).

pioner Digger or miner.

Here . . . The confused syntax indicates Hamlet's excitement; 'never' is the beginning of the oath. The sense is: Swear, here as before, that however strangely I may behave, you will never even hint that you know the reason why.

meet Suitable.

antic disposition Strange behaviour suggesting madness.

encumber'd Folded. Folded arms and head-shaking indicate dubiousness.

to note Hint.

fingers . . . The symbolic stance of discretion, which matches the folded arms and head-shaking of indiscretion described above.

out of joint Completely disordered. Notice how the traditional concluding rhyming couplet is here followed by another line, emphasizing the inconclusiveness, disorder and disturbance of the scene.

Revision questions on Act I

1 How does Shakespeare provide us with the information necessary to understand the main action of the play?

2 What is your impression of Hamlet's character at the end of Act I?

3 Make a list of the main images in this act and describe their importance in the play.

4 What do we learn about Polonius, Ophelia and Laertes in this act?

5 Why is Hamlet going to feign madness?

Act II Scene 1

Polonius instructs Reynaldo to spy on Laertes in Paris. Though shocked, Reynaldo agrees and departs. Ophelia enters in great distress, and tells her father about the visit she has just received from Hamlet. Polonius decides he has misjudged Hamlet and goes to tell Claudius about the incident.

The main point of this scene is to reveal the effects of Hamlet's new behaviour, and the inadequacy of Polonius's response, which contrasts ironically with his high estimate of his own powers. Ophelia describes Hamlet in what her father takes to be the classic guise of the demented lover (parodied in the character of Malvolio in *Twelfth Night*), ragged and dirty and distracted.

We are also introduced to the theme of spying and watching which pervades the play. The fraud and deceit of the court are made clear: Polonius is seen to conform to cynical sixteenth-century notions of the 'politician'; i.e. one who will do anything to achieve his ends. Even Reynaldo is shocked by the suggestion that he should deliberately lie and blacken Laertes' reputation. Polonius's instructions contrast ironically with Hamlet's reflections on honour and reputation at I,4,13ff.

The two halves of the scene show how both Polonius's children become pawns in his political game in different ways: Laertes watched and controlled at a distance, Ophelia subordinated to Claudius's interests.

Commentary

shall Would. Polonius's suggestion is really an order. Notice the fussy detail of the instructions, and the way in which the old man insists on Reynaldo's attention with 'Look you', 'mark this', etc and the irritating repetitions. Polonius is at once self-important and petty.

Marry A common interjection.

Danskers Danes.

keep Lodge.

encompassment Indirect way.

come . . . it You will come closer this way than by direct questions.

Take Assume.

forgeries Lies.

drabbing Whoring. Polonius is content to smear Laertes' reputation for his own 'good'. This meddling foreshadows his fatal interference in Hamlet's affairs.

dishonour Reynaldo seems to have a keener sense of truth and honour than his master.

season Modify.

another i.e. such as incontinency. The distinction between this and drabbing is spurious. Polonius uses it to brush off Reynaldo's inconvenient objections.

quaintly Skilfully.

unreclaimed Wild.

Of general assault Common to all men. The irony here is that Polonius urges Reynaldo to attribute to Laertes just that quality Laertes attributed to Hamlet (I,3,5–16) and which Hamlet thinks of as characteristic of Gertrude and Claudius, i.e. animal wildness and desire.

fetch of warrant Justified strategem. Polonius is a politician who thinks that ends justify means.

sullies Accusations.

As . . . working As though he were a little soiled in the process of acquiring his due accomplishments (as a gentleman).

party in converse Partner in conversation.

prenominate Aforementioned.

He . . . you He will agree with you.

addition Title. Polonius's long-windedness and fussiness are about to lead him into a muddle.

a He.

in's rouse In his cups.

Videlicet That is to say.

we . . . reach We wise and far-seeing people.

windlasses Indirect means.

assays of bias Devious attempts. This is Polonius's justification reiterated. Interestingly, Hamlet uses a 'bait of falsehood' in a different way when he sets up his play to trap the king (II,2,600).

my former lecture The lesson I have just given.

Observe . . . yourself Go along with his wishes. The following phrase means something similar.

unbrac'd Undone. Hamlet dresses to simulate madness. Compare 1,5,176–187.

foul'd Dirtied.

down-gyved Hanging round his ankles like fetters.

As if . . . Ophelia speaks truer than she knows.

Mad . . . Ironically they mistake the cause of Hamlet's madness.

Then goes . . . Then he holds me at arm's length.

As a As though he.

bulk Body. There is a certain comedy in this performance which smacks of over-acting – appropriate, perhaps, for a play in which acting plays such an important part.

property Nature.

fordoes Destroys.

I am sorry Polonius breaks off until l.111. Once again he does not follow through a train of thought.

quoted Watched.

I fear'd ... More irony. Polonius was wrong about Hamlet's 'trifling'. Now he's wrong about both the madness and its cause.

wrack Ruin.

beshrew A plague on. The whole speech is doubly ironic. In reproaching himself for getting it wrong the first time, Polonius now finds further grounds to esteem his own insight.

cast ... ourselves Be suspicious.

being ... love Keeping this secret might cause more grief than revealing it will cause hatred.

Act II Scene 2

The King welcomes Rosencrantz and Guildenstern whom he has summoned to help with Hamlet. Polonius announces the Norwegian ambassadors. When they depart he explains that Hamlet's behaviour is caused by love for Ophelia, and suggests to Claudius that they should spy on the lovers' meeting.

Hamlet meets Rosencrantz and Guildenstern who tell him about the arrival of the Players. He greets the Players and asks them to perform 'The Murder of Gonzago' before the King, including some extra lines by Hamlet himself.

This scene moves the action on in a number of ways, but its main interest depends on Hamlet's display of the 'antic disposition' promised in Act I Scene 5, and his encounter with the Players. Both involve the themes of appearance and performance which are central to the play's meaning. We have already encountered Claudius and Polonius pretending to be what they are not. Now Hamlet proposes to use their own weapon against them in two ways: indirectly, through his own dissembling, and directly through the staging of the play.

Commentary

sending Summoning. Compare this passage with II,1,1–75 and notice how much suaver Claudius is than Polonius. Both men seek their own ends under the cloak of benevolence.

Sith Since.

exterior ... was ... The antithesis here underlines the play's preoccupation with the conflicts between inner and outer, truth and show, appearance and reality.

What it should be ... Claudius must be curiously blind if this is really the case. More likely he prefers not to speculate in public on the relationship between Gertrude's remarriage and Hamlet's state of mind.

neighbour'd Intimate with.

draw him on Encourage him.

open'd Disclosed.

gentry Courtesy.

supply ... hope Satisfaction of our need.

dread Revered.

in ... bent Completely (a metaphor from archery).

some One.

our practices What we do. But there is a sense of 'practice' which involves guile or cunning, hence the irony of 'pleasant and helpful'.

still Ever.

duty ... King ... Polonius does not distinguish between his duty to God and his duty to the King – a common sentiment, and a dangerous one when the King is such as Claudius.

Hunts Follows. Ironically, Polonius turns out to be wrong, losing his life in consequence.

I ... marriage Gertrude is both right and wrong. She is right about the causes, but she doesn't yet know the extent of Claudius's guilt.

sift Interrogate.

Upon our first When we first raised the issue.

Polack King of Poland.

borne in hand Deceived.

sends ... Fortinbras Orders Fortinbras to stop.

assay Trial.

And ... time And when we have more time to consider it.

expostulate Examine. This speech is both a parody of the period's excessive rhetoric and a comic sample of Polonius at his worst – as the Queen impatiently hints at l.95. Observe the comic abruptness of 'Your son is mad' after the elaborate preparatory flourishes, which use the old rhetorical trick of saying 'I'll be brief' at great length. The comedy also derives from the tautologies (phrases which say the same thing in different words).

no art ... But this is just what Polonius uses in two senses: i) in his speech, and ii) in his attempts to manage Hamlet.

Perpend Consider. Polonius appears to have lost sight of what he is talking about. The whole series of Polonius's speeches from 86 to 151 boils down to 'Hamlet is mad because of his unrequited love for my daughter'.

mark Polonius uses the same fussy calls to attention as he did with Reynaldo.

To... What follows is as much a parody of an Elizabethan love-letter as Polonius's speech of an Elizabethan statesman. It even has the standard disclaimer 'I have not art...' This is certainly not the kind of letter we would expect Hamlet to write – which is precisely why it serves to deceive Polonius.

beautified Beautiful. Polonius fancies himself as a critic of style.

these i.e. this letter is addressed.

bosom Where a girl might keep her love letter.

am ... numbers Lack skill as a poet. These are indeed poor verses, but they do the job of fooling Polonius.

reckon (i) count (ii) express.

whilst ... him While this body is still his.

more above In addition.

fell out Occurred.

me Observe how Polonius is more concerned with his own standing than his daughter's circumstances.

I perceiv'd it This is a lie. See Act I Scene 3.

play'd ... book Acted as go-between.

given ... dumb Closed my eyes to it.

with idle sight Without noticing.

No... The whole speech is designed to elicit admiration for Polonius, but only confirms the audience in their contempt for this chattering fool.

round Directly.

my ... bespeak I had a word with madam.

out ... star Out of your reach.

prescripts Advice.

from his resort Out of his way.

took the fruits Experienced the results.

a short ... Such words from Polonius always bode hot air.

lightness Lightheadedness.

by this declension Decline in this way.

Hath there ... Polonius is filled with dangerous conceit.

Take this ... Ironic. Polonius's overconfidence in his own abilities results in death when he embarks on the plan described in l.163 below.

centre i.e. of the earth.

loose Release – but there is also a sexual connotation of looseness.

arras Tapestry.

thereon Because of it.

Let me ... Polonius harps obsessively on his own perceptiveness.

board Greet.

God-a-mercy God have mercy.

fishmonger This has the colloquial meaning of 'procurer'. We are getting our first direct taste of Hamlet's 'antic disposition', which encourages Polonius's delusion by means of the many sexual allusions. The comedy in the scene arises not only from the misunderstanding but from Polonius's belief that he is handling the situation well.

honest ... This word ironically refers the audience to Polonius's scheming.

carrion This can mean both dead flesh and live. The sun, like sexual kisses, is hot. The allusion is taken up three lines on. The references in these lines are all to fevered or disordered sexuality, suggesting Hamlet's supposed obsession with Ophelia.

Conception This can refer to the formation of ideas or to the conceiving of children. The second sense is repulsively linked with the notion of the sun 'breeding' maggots in carrion, not least because royalty is traditionally associated with the sun – so Hamlet is to Ophelia as the sun to carrion.

How ... that? What do you think of that?

fishmonger Polonius's dull literalism is his downfall. Anything remotely out of the ordinary he takes as madness.

in my youth ... The idea of comparing Hamlet and Polonius is comic in itself.

matter Polonius means 'subject', Hamlet means 'point at issue'.

old men ... This echoes the banal repetitions of Polonius's own speeches to the King and Queen. It also attacks him directly.

purging Discharging.

honesty Acceptable behaviour.

pregnant Apposite.

You cannot ... fools ... Hamlet moves through heavy irony to blunt rudeness.

indifferent Average. Notice how Hamlet switches back to sanity in his witty exchanges with the courtiers.

very Top. The three men play with clothing and body metaphors in the following lines.

privates Pun on private parts and ordinary citizens.

a strumpet Inconstant. Fortune is proverbially fickle.

there is nothing ... A commonplace contradicted by the action of the play in which there is a clear distinction between good (Old Hamlet) and bad (Claudius). The point here is that Hamlet is railing at the times – a conventional pastime in Elizabethan drama. His remarks are not important in themselves but for the state of mind they express.

the very ... dream We dream our ambitions before we realize them. Therefore, the realized ambition is the shadow or copy of something which is itself a shadow or copy of reality, as pointed out in the following lines.

Then are ... shadows Hamlet takes the idea to its limit. If ambition and its results are both the shadows of shadows, the only unshadowy beings are the unambitious (beggars) whose shadows are the ambitious (monarchs). The wearisome straining of the idea is both typical of Elizabethan rhetoric at its worst and suitable for the elaborately witty exchanges between these idle courtiers.

to the court... i.e. where such fanciful talk is in place.

reason... Unclear whether Hamlet means he's not up to this sort of thing (which is patently untrue) or whether he regards it as the very opposite of reasonable.

servants Hamlet plays on the other sense of 'wait upon'.

dreadfully attended Badly waited on – and also haunted by the Ghost.

beaten Familiar. Hamlet returns to common topics.

no...occasion Both true and false. They are visiting him with a purpose, as Hamlet suspects.

Anything... Hamlet speaks sarcastically – assuming they will conceal the truth.

colour Disguise. Their faces speak what their tongues conceal.

conjure Implore.

rights... The idea here is that friendship involves the right to mutual frankness.

consonancy Harmonious friendship. It isn't clear whether Hamlet is still speaking sarcastically.

a better proposer i.e. than Hamlet.

I...of you... I'm watching you.

hold not off Don't be backward.

prevent...discovery Come before your revelation.

moult no feather Remain unviolated.

lost...mirth... This is clearly untrue, to judge from his appearances so far. This famous speech is a set piece in which Hamlet presents himself to his friends in a melancholy light. He is not going to reveal the true reason for his strange state of mind, compounded of grief at his father's death, horror at the manner of it and his mother's remarriage, and elation at his newly-discovered sense of purpose. So he adopts the standard pose of the melancholy man – just as he adopted the standard pose of the deranged lover with Polonius. Hamlet, as we are about to discover, is a lover of the theatre and a player of parts. The smiling of his friends (l.310) acknowledges the lightness of his tone. Which is not to say there is no serious undercurrent to Hamlet's words – only that we must beware of taking them too literally, like Polonius.

frame Structure.

fretted Ornamented.

infinite See l.255.

express Perfectly shaped.

angel...god Here we return to the imagery associated with Hamlet's father, this time balanced against the quintessence of dust, i.e. the very essence of the base material.

Lenten Meagre.

the players . . . The arrival of the players signals to the audience the writer's high level of self-consciousness. They will act a play of just the sort *Hamlet* itself might have been, had Shakespeare not transcended this kind of melodrama. Nevertheless, his own acquaintance with the type – and his delight in its excesses – are apparent in the encounter that follows.

coted Overtook.

tribute on Tribute from.

target Shield.

the humorous . . . Not the comic but one ruled by the humours – somewhat like Hamlet himself, perhaps.

whose . . . th'sear Who laugh easily.

the lady Every company contains stock roles: the king, the knight, the lady, etc.

inhibition Repression.

Innovation Rebellion. There may be a contemporary allusion here. The players have been sent on their travels by some sort of political upheaval – another detail pointing to the unsettled times in Denmark.

estimation Reputation.

wonted pace Usual way.

eyrie Nest, here meaning 'company'.

eyases Young hawks, i.e. boy actors. They threaten to put the other companies out of business. The public enjoyed seeing the different troupes attacking one another, which intensified the rivalry.

on . . . question Aggressively.

tryannically Enthusiastically.

berattle Attack.

goose-quills Pens.

escotted Supported.

Will . . . sing? Will they continue to act only until their voices break?

common players Ordinary actors.

if . . . better If they have no better way of making a living.

exclaim . . . succession Criticize what they will themselves become when they grow up.

tar Encourage.

bid for argument Paid for performance. Argument also means plot.

in the question About the issue (of child actors v. 'common players').

brains Ideas – but the phrase also hints at violence.

carry it away Prevail.

his load The world – which Hercules is said to carry on his shoulders.

make mouths Pull faces, criticize.

little Miniature. Claudius, like the boy actors, is in the fashion for no very good reason.

philosophy Enquiry.

Gentlemen Hamlet here addresses Rosencrantz and Guildenstern, somewhat grudgingly, it seems. Though they are supposed to be old friends, he is careful to give them proper formal welcome before the Players arrive. On the one hand he doesn't want them to feel slighted; on the other, he is suspicious.

Th'appurtenance The proper manner.

comply ... garb Give you the appropriate reception.

extent Behaviour.

should ... yours Should seem more favourable than your welcome.

uncle-father ... Hamlet speaks bluntly and ironically of his 'parents' here.

north-north-west Only sometimes. Hamlet hints that he knows what is going on.

Well be with you Welcome.

at each ear One on either side.

Happily Perhaps.

You say ... indeed ... Hamlet feigns to be deep in talk.

Roscius The most renowned actor of classical times. The relevance is obvious; Hamlet teases Polonius.

Buzz A rudely dismissive comment.

Seneca Roman tragedian.

Plautus Roman comic writer.

law ... liberty This phrase appears to refer to Plautus, who writes with the freedom or liberty of the comedian, and Seneca who conforms to the rules or 'law' of tragic drama.

Jepthah Jepthah sacrificed his only daughter, a virgin, in fulfilment of a vow to God (Judges xi,29–40). There are two levels of irony in this reference: (i) Hamlet hints at the contrast with the fishmonger (see l.174); (ii) Polonius will unknowingly sacrifice his daughter later in the play.

One fair daughter ... Hamlet quotes from a contemporary ballad, here and at l.411 below.

passing Very.

row Stanza.

abridgement ... The entry of the Players cuts short Hamlet's teasing.

valanced Covered with a beard.

my young lady ... Hamlet is addressing the actor who played the female roles. There were no actresses.

nearer to heaven Taller.

chopine Shoe.

cracked ... ring Hamlet hopes the boy's voice is not yet broken and therefore unsuitable for women's parts. This elaborate metaphor refers to the practice of clipping the edges off coins for the spare metal, devaluing them as legal tender once they were clipped (or cracked) beyond the ring surrounding the sovereign's head. But there is a further hint at the comparison between a cracked coin and a woman's cracked (lost) virginity.

e'en to't Do our best.

quality Ability.

general Mob.

 received Understood.

cried ... mine Corroborated from their superior understanding.

digested Arranged.

modesty Restraint. This is ironic, in view of what follows.

sallets Tasty, i.e. saucy, bits.

affection Affectation.

handsome ... fine Naturally attractive rather than cleverly constructed.

Aeneas ... Dido On his way from the devastated Troy to found a new city (Rome) in Italy, Aeneas stopped in Carthage where he had a passionate affair with Queen Dido, who killed herself on his departure. Aeneas is the son of Priam, King of Troy, slain by Pyrrhus. Among Shakespeare's contemporaries, both Marlowe and Nashe wrote plays on the subject of Dido and Aeneas.

The rugged ... Shakespeare here parodies the elaborate, bombastic style of contemporary tragedy for a serious purpose. For more on this, see the commentary below on Hamlet's concluding soliloquy.

Hyrcanian beast Tiger.

sable arms Black armour.

ominous horse This is the wooden horse in which the Greeks secretly entered Troy.

complexion Appearance.

heraldry Heraldic colour. The heraldic colours were black (sable) and red (gules). The first is almost completely smeared with the second, i.e. blood.

 dismal Threatening.

trick'd Marked. Another heraldic term.

impasted with Dried to a paste by.

lend Give.

o'ersized Covered.

Rebellious to Not obeying. This sort of grandiose construction is typical of the speech which is meant to be thrillingly grand. 'Repugnant to' means the same.

whiff and wind ... fell i.e. even the hissing of the deadly sword was enough to kill. Deadly.

unnerved Feeble.

senseless Unfeeling – but nevertheless it seems to feel.

 Ilium The citadel of Troy.

Stoops ... base Falls.

Takes ... ear Pyrrhus is distracted by the noise of crashing Ilium.

declining Descending.

milky White-haired.

like . . . will and matter Indifferent to his desire and its object.

against Before.

rack Clouds.

region Sky.

Cyclops One-eyed metal-working giants in Roman and Greek mythology.

Mars Roman god of war.

proof eterne Eternal strength.

strumpet Fortune See note to l.235.

fellies Rims.

nave Hub. The Goddess Fortuna is traditionally represented as spinning a wheel to which all men are tied. When they are carried up by the wheel they have good fortune; when down, bad.

as low as . . . i.e. down to Hell.

too long It is pretty cheeky of Polonius to say this.

beard The sign of Polonius's wagging chin. Hamlet is telling him to shut up.

tale of bawdry Saucy story. Hamlet teases Polonius again.

Hecuba The wife of King Priam.

mobbled With muffled face.

bisson rheum Blinding tears.

clout Cloth.

all o'erteemed Worn out (with child-bearing).

milch . . . Moist. Even the gods would have wept to see Hecuba in this state.

whe'er Whether. It is the Player who weeps in his telling.

abstract Summary.

according . . . desert As they deserve.

after According to.

for a need If necessary.

mock him not . . . Hamlet doesn't want the Players to follow his example.

God buy Goodbye.

alone . . . In this soliloquy Hamlet contrasts the Player's passionate response to an imaginary situation with his own sluggishness. He then explains his scheme to shame the king by simulating the murder of Old Hamlet in a play.

peasant Base.

conceit Conception.

wann'd paled.

function Demeanour. The idea is that everything about the player expresses what he imagines.

Make mad . . . The Elizabethans had a vivid sense of drama's emotional impact under ordinary circumstances. This is not ordinary.

free Innocent.

muddy-mettled Dull-spirited.

 peak Mope.

unpregnant of . . . i.e. not producing any action in response to his 'cause'.

property This may refer to Gertrude.

defeat Successful attack.

pate Head. The following actions are all ritualized challenges.

As . . . lungs . . . The deeper the lie's source the worse its nature.

'Swounds God's wounds – a common oath.

I . . . it I should accept the charge of cowardice.

pigeon-liver'd Proverbially meek. The gall is supposedly the source of bitter feelings.

oppression Distress.

all . . . kites All the kites in the district. Kites are carrion birds.

this slave . . . i.e. Claudius.

brave Admirable. Hamlet speaks ironically, reproaching himself for resorting to words when he should be doing something.
 Appropriately, he then decides upon a plan of action which depends upon words – but also on a dumb-show.

heaven and hell See note on I,5,92–3.

scullion Kitchen servant.

About Come on!

proclaim'd Admitted in public.

no tongue . . . So the dumb-show's silence is appropriate.

tent Probe.

blench Squirm.

The spirit . . . Here Hamlet offers one possible motive for his hesitancy.

relative Convincing.

Revision questions on Act II

1 What is the function of the Players in this act?

2 Summarize Hamlet's speech beginning 'I will tell you why' in scene 2.

3 Pick out any comic moments in the act and say what they contribute to the play.

4 Explain Hamlet's final soliloquy and its significance. Why does it come where it does?

5 What is the point of having Rosencrantz and Guildenstern in the play?

Act III Scene 1

The King questions Rosencrantz and Guildenstern about Hamlet's state of mind. He learns little. Polonius announces the play and conveys Hamlet's invitation to the King and Queen for that night.

Hamlet enters, brooding on his situation, and the King and Polonius spy on his conversation with Ophelia, in which he is grossly offensive. The King, convinced that Hamlet's condition means danger to himself, decides to send the prince to England. The main point of this scene dramatically is not Hamlet's famous soliloquy ('To be or not to be') but the encounter with Ophelia which is watched by Polonius and the King. They, together with Rosencrantz and Guildenstern, have tried to fathom Hamlet and failed. Now Ophelia is set to the task, and thus betrayed by her father who uses his own daughter to please Claudius and raise himself in the King's estimation. The scene is therefore an important stage in the central struggle between the prince and his uncle – and, ironically, in the downfall of Polonius and his family. It also reveals Claudius's uneasiness, and his virtual admission of guilt (ll.49–53).

Commentary

drift of conference Way of talking. Compare Polonius's advice to Reynaldo in II.1.

puts on ... As this speech begins with 'And', indicating a conversation in progress, the courtiers have presumably told Claudius about Hamlet's claim that he is only sometimes mad – and suspects that the lunacy is assumed.

distracted Confused. This is not, of course, the same as being mad.

crafty madness See note on l.2 above.

forcing ... See note on II,2,366.

assay him to Try to persuade him to take part in.

o'erraught Overtook.

edge Encouragement. The King's enthusiasm to see the play is ironic.

drive his purpose Urge him on.

Affront Encounter.

espials Spies. Their lawfulness is dubious.

bestow Conceal.

the happy cause ... i.e. rather than Gertrude's own marriage.

Gracious Addressed to the King.

exercise Devotion.

colour your loneliness Provide a reason for your solitude. Presumably necessary because Ophelia is normally kept strictly away from Hamlet.

sugar o'er Another image of conflicting appearance and reality which comes ironically from Polonius. The King takes up the idea, giving the first clear hint of his guilt.

painted The words paint a false picture, as the harlot 'paints on' her beauty.

To be ... Shakespeare's (and Hamlet's) most famous single speech. Opinion is divided about the meaning, some readers seeing the theme as suicide, others the consequence of action. It depends on what we make of Hamlet's state of mind at this stage of the play. The question may be: 'Do I want to go on living?' or it may be: 'Shall I just put up quietly with the present situation, or fight it and die as a result?' If we take the second alternative, the opening question becomes not 'To kill myself or not?' but 'To survive or not?'.

suffer Endure.

outrageous Unpredictable.

end them Some commentators claim this means 'be ended by them'. See discussion above.

No more i.e. death is no more than sleep.

consummation Fulfilment.

rub Difficulty. Hamlet had already referred to his troublesome dreams.

coil Turmoil.

respect Consideration.

dispriz'd Unvalued.

quietus Settlement.

bodkin Dagger. It is unclear whether Hamlet intends the dagger for himself or for Claudius. See the first note on this speech, above.

fardels Burdens.

bourn Boundary.

puzzles Paralyses.

conscience Closer to modern 'consciousness' than to our sense of 'moral obligation'.

native hue Red: the colour associated with resolution. The image is continued in 'pale cast'.

pitch Loftiness.

With this regard Because of this.

Soft you Be quiet.

orisons Prayers. But Ophelia isn't really praying, as we know, so the reference is ironic. Compare III,3,36ff.

remembrances Tokens.

redeliver Give back.

aught Hamlet is here denying that there was ever anything between them, not that he never wrote to her or gave presents.

you know right well Ophelia refuses to accept his disclaimer.

sweet breath The sweet intention of the words is transferred to the breath.

Take . . . unkind An example of the sententious saying in a couplet, common in this play and the drama of the time generally.

honest Frequently has the meaning of chaste. Hamlet questions Ophelia aggressively.

admit . . . to Allow no discourse with.

Could beauty . . . Hamlet means that Ophelia's chastity should prevent her from allowing any man to view her beauty too intimately. Ophelia takes up the word-play, pointing out that honesty/chastity and beauty are rightly linked.

Ay, truly . . . Hamlet claims that (sexual) beauty both seduces others and encourages them to destroy chastity; whereas the chaste do not easily persuade the beautiful, i.e. desirable, to be like themselves.

but . . . relish it But we still show our true natures. A small dose of virtue doesn't innoculate Hamlet against his true instincts – or so he says.

I loved you not It wasn't really love I felt for you.

nunnery . . . Where she can preserve her chastity. But nunnery was also slang for brothel.

indifferent honest Fairly honest/chaste.

We i.e. all men.

this plague i.e. curse.

monsters Cuckolds.

your paintings . . . The speech which follows is standard sixteenth-century raillery at the expense of women. 'Paint' is make-up.

jig and amble Walk in a seductive way.

make . . . ignorance Pretend that your lasciviousness is really naïvety.

mad . . . It is impossible to tell how far Hamlet has worked himself into a real temper and how far his abuse is assumed. Critics often connect this treatment of Ophelia with the prince's distress over his mother's remarriage, but there is no obvious connection.

all but one i.e. Claudius – who is listening.

expectancy Future.

rose Symbol of perfect beauty.

glass . . . form Model for others.

observ'd i.e. the one everybody watches.

music vows Vows like music. The image is continued at l.160. Harmony is a common image for the well-ordered mind.

feature of blown Shape of full-blown.

ecstasy Madness. Ophelia assumes that Hamlet must be mad to speak so. His stratagem – if such it was – has worked.

lack'd form ... Claudius has a juster estimate of Hamlet's condition than Ophelia does.

sits on brood i.e. like a bird on eggs. Claudius rightly sees the likely result. Compare II,2,563.

hatch Continuing the metaphor.

set it down Decided.

tribute The Danegeld, money paid by native Britons to their Danish conquerors in the tenth century. By implication, any kind of protection money.

This ... heart Whatever it is that has a grip on Hamlet's feelings. The King must have a shrewd idea by now that this 'something' involves himself – without knowing the full truth.

fashion of himself His usual behaviour.

neglected love ... Polonius has too high an estimate of his own insight to let go of the first notion. But there is also irony here: he doesn't know what Claudius, Hamlet and the audience know.

round Direct.

in the ear ... Polonius cannot resist this unnecessary spying, with fatal consequences. Note the ear image which runs through the play. What people hear and see – when sometimes they shouldn't – plays a vital role.

find him not Doesn't get to the bottom of it.

Act III Scene 2

Hamlet explains to the Players what he wants them to do. He asks Polonius to summon the King and Queen while Rosencrantz and Guildenstern ready the Players; and tells Horatio to watch the King carefully during the performance. When Claudius and his retinue enter, Hamlet once again assumes his 'antic disposition', taunting Polonius and Ophelia until the play begins – first the dumb-show, then the play proper. At the moment when Lucianus poisons the sleeping figure, Claudius rises and hurries out, followed by the Court. The Queen sends for Hamlet who has further talk with Rosencrantz and Guildenstern, and the scene ends with a soliloquy in which Hamlet restates his firm intention to seek revenge, but to be gentle with his mother, as instructed by the Ghost.

This scene, which is the turning point in the play, provides public confirmation of Claudius's guilt which it enacts, paradoxically thereby providing a prologue to *Hamlet* in the middle of the play: we see the scene the Ghost described. Claudius has already admitted his guilt in an aside (in the previous scene): we know that he is in a vulnerable state of mind.

The Players perform a drama which is in marked contrast to Shakespeare's own. The verse is formal, stately and monotonous, the sentiments commonplace, the phrases often painfully elaborate.

Commentary

your players Players in general.

as lief Rather.

robustious Ranting.

periwig-pated Bewigged.

groundlings Spectators in the cheapest part of the theatre.

are capable of Relish.

Termagant A stock dramatic figure, aggressive and noisy.

Herod The biblical king, always presented as violent.

modesty of nature Imitation of reality.

is from Departs from.

feature Appearance.

pressure Shape (from impression).

come tardy off Badly performed.

unskilful Undiscerning.

journeymen Assistants.

indifferently Somewhat.

set on Encourage.

barren Stupid.

though ... considered The sense here is that bad clowns get cheap laughs at the expense of obscuring important moments in the play.

uses it Does it.

presently At once.

As ... withal As I have ever come across in my dealings with others.

candied i.e. flattering.

pregnant Ready.

thrift Profit.

could ... election Was capable of making a choice among men.

Sh'ath She (the soul) has.

Fortune's buffets ... See the note on III,1,55ff. Having reflected on the pains of life Hamlet now characterizes the man who can bear them.

blood Feeling or passion.

commeddled Mingled.

passion's slave ... Hamlet appears to be indirectly recommending such an approach to life for himself.

something . . . Hamlet reminds himself to come to the point.

very comment Most penetrating examination.

occulted Hidden.

in one speech At one speech – the one added by Hamlet.

Vulcan The smith among Roman gods whose smithy is therefore black and hellish.

Give . . . note Pay close attention to him (Claudius).

censure . . . seeming Judgement of his behaviour.

idle i.e. not seen conspiring with Horatio.

chameleon's dish . . . Chameleons were supposed to feed on air. Hamlet takes Claudius's 'fares' to mean 'eats' not 'does'.

I have nothing I understand nothing – but also, I have no connection with.

now i.e. because they have been spoken and vanished.

capital a calf Excellent a fool.

attractive i.e. like a magnet.

in your lap The phrase is suggestive when addressed to a woman.

country matters Sexual intercourse.

fair Both 'pleasing' and 'pure'.

Nothing i.e. the absence of the penis. Hamlet veers between courtly wit and vulgarity.

jig-maker Comic writer.

sables Dark fur, but also black in heraldry.

two months . . . Hamlet ignores Ophelia's 'twice two months'.

by'r lady By Our Lady (the Virgin Mary).

hobby-horse Proverbially forgotten.

miching malicho Cunning mischief.

imports the argument Conveys the plot.

by From.

keep counsel Keep secret. It is in the very nature of acting to display. Hamlet has been keeping his counsel – which they will now divulge for him.

show . . . show Hamlet hints that Ophelia may 'show' herself sexually. She angrily rebukes him in l.143.

naught Worthless, good for nothing.

posy Motto.

Phoebus' cart The sun. Phoebus is the sun god in Roman mythology.

Neptune's salt-wash The sea. Neptune is the sea god.

Tellus' orbed ground The earth.

Hymen The god of marriage.

bands Bonds.

distrust you Worry about you.

hold quantity Match one another.

in . . . extremity Lacking both or experiencing both in extremes. The Player Queen's style recalls Polonius.

operant Active.

leave to do No longer work.

None wed . . . first This doesn't mean that a second marriage always implies actual murder, but that it is a kind of murder (i.e. rejection) of the first spouse to take another. The idea is made explicit at ll.179–80.

wormwood Bitter (to Gertrude).

instances Motives.

move Produce.

respects Considerations.

Purpose . . . memory Because without memory it diminishes.

validity Strength.

To pay . . debt Our good intentions are, in a sense, only debts to ourselves, and usually remain unpaid (i.e. unfulfilled), when we forget them. The wearisome elaboration of this idea through more than ten lines of poor rhyming couplets provides a comic interlude with a deadly serious purpose.

fortune Another meditation on the goddess.

anchor Anchorite or hermit.

cheer Fare.

scope Fate.

Each . . . destroy May everything I want to do well be destroyed by what opposes it, thus draining the happiness from my face.

hence In the next world. Notice the formal inversions which complicate this speech by turning the sentences round.

fain . . . beguile I would gladly while away.

protest i.e. protest her devotion. The Queen might well say this.

she'll . . . i.e. in contrast to Gertrude.

Have . . . argument Do you know the plot? Either the King hasn't paid attention to the dumbshow, or his question is a nervous tic.

jest Show. Hamlet's heavy irony contrasts this appearance with the reality of his uncle's crime and his mother's betrayal.

The Mousetrap As we know (from II,2,532) the play is actually called The Murder of Gonzago; but for Hamlet it is the trap in which he will catch (II,2,600) 'the conscience of the king'.

tropically Figuratively speaking.

knavish Wicked.

galled jade Sore, worn horse.

withers . . . unwrung Neckjoints are not wrenched.

a chorus An actor within a play who interprets it for the audience.

I . . . dallying i.e. I could supply the conversation between you and your lover if I could see the puppets being manipulated. Hamlet here tells Ophelia that he knows she is controlled by her father.

keen Bitter.

It . . . edge A double meaning here on 'edge' which means both 'sharp tongue' and 'desire'.

better and worse Even wittier and more indecent. Ophelia doesn't let Hamlet get away with his remarks, though she has no ripostes.

mis-take A woman takes her husband 'for better for worse'. 'Your' refers to any woman here.

Confederate Conspiring.

else no No other.

rank Foul-smelling.

Hecate's . . . blasted Damned three times by the curse of Hecate (goddess associated with witchcraft).

On . . . usurps Takes possession of.

estate Means both 'property' and 'rank'.

false fire Unloaded guns.

ungalled Uninjured. Claudius is the stricken deer – but so, of course, is Hamlet, which makes his song ironic. 'Watch' and 'sleep' in l.267 may refer to Hamlet and his father.

this i.e. this play.

forest . . . shoes Refers to the gaudy costumes of actors.

turn Turk Become unbelievers, i.e. let me down.

cry Company (as of hounds).

half a share Shareholding actors in companies were superior to hired hands. In the next line Hamlet claims a full share.

Damon A reference to Damon and Pythias, two proverbially close friends.

dismantled Deprived. Hamlet compares his father to Jove.

pajock An insulting nonsense-word, substituting for the word Horatio expects: 'ass'.

belike Perhaps.

distempered Upset.

choler Anger.

to the doctor . . . Because choler can also mean 'bile', acid stomach.

purgation This can mean either physical or spiritual cleansing. Hamlet continues his obsessive word-play and irony.

frame Form.

start Jump.

my affair What I'm saying.

wholesome Reasonable.

We . . . The royal 'we'.

pickers and stealers Hands.

advancement Taken with Hamlet's next speech, this appears to be a pun. The meaning for Rosencrantz's sake is 'promotion' – by which claim Rosencrantz is rightly surprised. But Hamlet also implies he is not getting on far enough with his revenge.

proverb . . . 'While the grass grows the horse starves.'

withdraw Speak privately.

to . . . toil An obscure metaphor from hunting which refers to the practice of driving quarry into nets against the wind, lest they smell the hunter. Rosencrantz is accused of hiding his true intentions as the hunter hides his smell.

if ... unmannerly ... If Hamlet cannot understand this, how can we?

I ... it I don't know how to play it.

lying An obvious allusion to their deceit. Hamlet makes a comparison between performing soothing music and telling lies. His former friends continue to deny their skill in either.

Govern ... ventages Control these holes.

stops Holes.

'Sblood By God's blood.

Then In that case. The inconsequence is part of his fooling.

top of my bent To extreme lengths.

thy nature i.e. as a son.

Nero A notoriously savage Roman emperor who had his mother murdered.

shent Censured.

To ... seals i.e. my soul would never consent to confirm my words with actions.

Act III Scene 3

Claudius makes his preparations for dispatching Hamlet to England. Polonius announces his intention to eavesdrop on Hamlet's conversation with Gertrude. Alone, Claudius kneels to pray, but cannot. Hamlet, passing secretly by, decides not to kill him yet.

Although this scene elaborates a little further the sub-plot of Hamlet's journey to England with Rosencrantz and Guildenstern, its main purpose is the ironic contrast between Claudius, unable to pray, and Hamlet unwilling to strike while the King is apparently at prayer. Previously the King has spied on Hamlet without success. Now Hamlet does the same to Claudius, enhancing the feeling that everyone is nervously watching everyone else – but without much effect. Polonius's promise to return later to tell the King what he has learnt (l.34) becomes ironic in this context: not only does Polonius learn nothing, he dies for his pains. The theme of the difference between appearance and reality is nowhere more ironically developed.

Commentary

nor . . . safe Nor is it safe for me. Ironically, Hamlet's plan has worked so well it now threatens to backfire. The King cannot brazen things out: he must dispose of his nephew.

forthwith dispatch Make ready at once.

The . . . estate My situation as king.

Out . . . brows In his head.

provide Prepare.

fear it is Dread which causes us. They claim to go along with Claudius's scheme for the sake of Denmark.

peculiar Private.

noyance Damage.

weal Welfare. Rosencrantz elaborates an argument which pervades the play: the well-being of the state depends upon the monarch. By the same token, a bad ruler makes an ill state.

cess Death. Ironically, these lines might be applied to Old Hamlet.

gulf Whirlpool.

mortis'd Jointed.

annexment Attachment.

Arm you Prepare yourselves. The sense of urgency is constantly reiterated.

fear Thing to be feared, i.e. Hamlet. Compare this talk of chaining Hamlet with his own sense of imprisonment at II,2,243.

process Proceedings.

tax him home Criticize him severely.

as you said . . . It was Polonius's idea.

nature Compare this use with 'unnatural' at III,3,386.

of vantage In addition.

my offence . . . Here Claudius reveals the anguish under the smooth surface.

rank . . . The foul-smellingness of evil is a recurrent image in the play.

primal eldest . . . Referring to the quarrel of Cain and Abel.

double business Two enterprises.

neglect . . . Ironically, this compares with Hamlet's own delay.

confront . . . offence Overcome the face of guilt.

forestalled Prevented.

fall . . . i.e. into sin.

look up . . . The irony is that Claudius can look up to Heaven but cannot find the will fully to atone for his sin by giving up its fruits.

th'offence The fruits of the crime.

corrupted currents Wicked ways.

shove by Push aside. The sense of the sentence is that the profits of sin can themselves be used to evade justice.

shuffling Trickery – with a clear echo of the previous 'shove by', emphasizing the difference between earthly and heavenly justice.

lies Appears.

In . . . forehead Without any concealment.

rests Remains.

can Can do. Notice how Claudius moves uneasily between hope and despair here.

limed Stuck – birds are trapped more completely as they struggle in bird-lime.

assay Effort.

pat Without delay. The repetition of 'now' underlines his decision – which is immediately contradicted in a dramatic turn-round. If he kills Claudius while praying, the King's soul may be absolved and go to Heaven. What he doesn't know, is that Claudius finds himself unable to pray: he only appears to do so.

would be scann'd Must be thought about.

hire and salary . . . i.e. because Claudius might be expected to reward him.

full of bread A biblical allusion signifying indulgence in sinful pleasure. See I,5,76–7.

broad blown In full blossom.

flush Full of vitality.

But . . . thought To our understanding.

season'd Prepared.

hent Moment.

relish Trace.

heels may kick . . . A vivid image of Claudius hurtling down to hell.

stays Waits.

physic Medicine.

My words . . . Claudius's last couplet underlines the irony of Hamlet's decision.

Act III Scene 4

As Hamlet enters his mother's room, Polonius hides behind the arras. Son and mother talk and Hamlet becomes increasingly agitated. When Gertrude calls out in alarm, Polonius answers. Hamlet, taking him to be the King, stabs him through the arras. As he continues to criticize Gertrude, the Ghost enters, urging him to action. He tells his mother his madness is a pretence and begs her to give up Claudius.

This scene contrasts with the previous one in two important ways. First, Gertrude (unlike Claudius) shows signs of true repentance. Second, Hamlet kills Polonius by mistake, having not killed Claudius when he could.

This is the only scene in the play in which Hamlet and his mother have an extended discussion – if Hamlet's attack on Gertrude can be called such – and it marks another turning point in the action when the Queen, smitten by remorse for her association with Claudius, agrees to support Hamlet's deception. This seems to mean that all the major characters in the play are deceiving someone. The Queen's consent is brought about by her recognition that Hamlet is right in his insistence that she should not have married Claudius. But notice how Hamlet dwells on this point. Although he calls Claudius a murderer, he does not specify the murder of Old Hamlet. He criticizes Gertrude not for complicity in murder but for her marriage to an inferior man who is her former husband's brother. The whole emphasis of the scene is on the imagery of sexual disgust. It is feeling, not justice, which prevails here, with both Hamlet and his mother.

Commentary

lay . . . him Be firm with him. Polonius orders the Queen about.
been too broad Gone too far.
round Plain-spoken.
my father . . . i.e. Old Hamlet. Hamlet calls his mother 'you', she calls him 'thou': his term is respectful and defiant, hers intimate.
rood Cross.
a ducat i.e. the value of the life which Hamlet takes to be Claudius's (see l.32 below). The contrast between his haste here and the delay in the previous scene is striking.
kill a king? Gertrude's question implies her innocence.
it . . . word That's what I said.
Thou find'st . . . Hamlet says the appropriate epitaph on Polonius.
damned custom Evil habits.
proof Impermeable.
 sense Feeling.
rose The symbol of pure love and beauty.
contraction Engagement.
glow Blush.
solidity . . . mass Earth.
as . . . doom In expectation of the day of judgement.
Is And is. In this speech Hamlet makes the Queen's adultery of cosmic significance, as he did with his father's murder. Notice also the sexual charge in much of the language.

index Introduction – just as the index came at the beginning of a book.

picture . . . Recalling Hamlet's original comparison in I,2.

front of Jove The forehead of Jove (King of the Gods).

Mars God of war.

station Bearing.

Mercury Winged messenger of the gods – and therefore graceful and light-footed.

heaven-kissing Contrast the language here with ll.40–51.

a man See I,2,187.

husband Reiterating the word emphasizes the comparison. Compare ll.8–11 above.

ear i.e. of corn. But the reminiscence of Claudius's crime is irresistible.

blasting Withering.

leave to feed Stop feeding. Compare III,3,10.

heyday Excitement (from 'hey-day' meaning holiday).

Sense Faculties of sense. Note the play with 'sense' and 'sure'.

apoplex'd Paralysed.

err i.e. err so much.

ecstasy Excitement.

such a difference i.e. between the brothers.

cozen'd Cheated.

hoodman-blind Blind man's buff.

Eyes . . . This refers back to ll.71, playfully linking the senses.

so mope Be so foolish.

her own fire i.e. youth's.

frost i.e. the older woman's passion compared with the girl's.

panders Assists.

grained Ingrained.

tinct Colour.

enseamed Greasy.

daggers See III,2,387.

tithe Tenth.

vice The devil's sidekick in morality plays.

cutpurse Thief.

he's mad Gertrude cannot see or hear the Ghost.

laps'd . . . passion This can mean either that Hamlet has let both time and passion (for revenge) slip away, or that he has wasted time in passionate reproaches.

important acting Urgent fulfilment.

amazement Bewilderment.

Conceit Imagination.

Alas . . . Gertrude turns the verbal tables on her son. Compare l.9.

as . . . th'alarm Like sleeping soldiers called to arms.

bedded Smoothed.

excrements Outgrowths (such as hair).

distemper Upset.

conjoin'd Together.

capable Capable of feeling.

piteous action i.e. the Ghost's request of mercy for Gertrude.

effects Intentions.

will ... colour Will lose its proper character.

habit Usual clothes.

coinage Invention.

This ... in Madness is very cunning in creating such an illusion.

gambol Jump away.

unction ointment.

all within ... The theme of hidden corruption permeates the play.

ranker ... Rank weeds, the disordered garden, are persistent images.

my virtue ... i.e. his harsh plain-speaking.

pursy Flabby.

Assume Practise.

doth eat ... i.e. and thus remove.

frock or livery Uniform. The point Hamlet makes is that just as custom blunts our sense of evil, so it can help us cultivate good habits.

stamp of nature Inclination.

same lord i.e. Polonius.

To ... me To punish me by making me responsible for this murder, and to make me the agency of Polonius's death.

their The heavens'.

bestow Dispose of.

answer Explain.

cruel ... Hamlet's theme throughout the scene.

behind To come.

Not this ... Hamlet speaks ironically. He is telling the Queen not to reveal his secret.

bloat Puffy.

wanton Wantonly.

reechy Reeking.

paddling Fondling. Hamlet's disgust becomes almost hysterical here.

ravel ... out Disentangle.

'Twere good ... The heavy irony continues.

paddock ... gib Toad ... cat.

Dear concernings Important matters.

Unpeg ... What follows is generally thought to refer to a fable, signifying that for Gertrude to reveal Hamlet's secret (open the basket) will be as fatal to her as the ape's attempt to imitate birds in the fable.

try conclusions Experiment.

down By falling.

knavery The results of knavery.

hoist Blown up.
petard Bomb. Hamlet foretells his success in turning his former
  friends' mission against them.
and't ... will It will go badly if I don't.
crafts Plots.
packing i) plotting, ii) hurrying.
This ... grave Hamlet ironically lists a counsellor's appropriate
  qualities.

Revision questions on Act III

1 Give a detailed summary of 'To be, or not to be ...' What state
of mind is Hamlet in when he delivers the speech?

2 What happens to Ophelia in Act III?

3 Are the characters of Claudius and Gertrude developed any
further in this act?

4 How justified is Hamlet in killing Polonius, and what is his
attitude to Polonius's death?

5 Explain the different uses of prose and verse in this act.

Act IV Scene 1

The Queen tells Claudius about Polonius's death. He realizes
Hamlet's sword was meant for him and wonders about the effect
on the populace. Rosencrantz and Guildenstern are set to watch
Hamlet until they leave the country, which is to be as soon as
possible.

The first four short scenes of this act forward the action. Now
Hamlet has murdered Polonius he is temporarily at his uncle's
mercy. Realizing that his nephew means business, Claudius
begins to evolve a scheme for disposing of him. But the net is
closing. Polonius is now dead, and Gertrude is secretly carrying
out Hamlet's instruction to support his pretence of madness.

Commentary

Bestow ... us Leave us alone.
Mad ... Gertrude does Hamlet's bidding.
brainish Crazed.
answer'd Dealt with.

providence Foresight.
short Tethered.
  out of haunt Away from others.
divulging Becoming known.
pith Vital part. Once again the image of disease eating away at a
  hidden core.
mineral Mine.
As . . . blank As straight as the cannon to its target.
woundless Which cannot be wounded.

Act IV Scene 2

Putting on his antic disposition Hamlet refuses to say where the
body is, but agrees to go to the King. He is now completely
alienated from his former friends, Rozencrantz and Guildenstern.

Commentary

counsel Secret.
demanded of Questioned by.
replication Reply.
countenance Favour.
mouthed In his mouth. It is Claudius who resembles the ape.
gleaned Learned. Hamlet tells them that Claudius will push them aside
  once they have served their turn.
with the King In the palace. But Claudius is not yet 'with the body'
  because he is still alive.
nothing No account.

Act IV Scene 3

The King is now desperate to be rid of Hamlet, who treats his
enquiries about Polonius with ironic contempt. Claudius
informs the prince that he is to be sent to England for his own
safety, because of his unpopularity with the people. As Hamlet
leaves, Claudius begs Rosencrantz and Guildenstern to hurry –
but this is all for public consumption: when they leave, Claudius
reveals the plan to have Hamlet killed the moment he arrives in
England.

Commentary

distracted Muddle-headed.

Who ... eyes Who judge not by their reason but by appearances.

scourge Punishment.

Deliberate pause The result of consideration.

appliance Remedy.

politic i) Shrewd, ii) discreet.

Your worm ... A complicated conceit. The worm is an emperor because he feeds on those who feed on others. But 'diet' (like 'convocation') is also a kind of council.

but variable service Only different dishes.

progress Ceremonial journey.

yourself ... A heavy hint.

nose Smell.

tender Care for.

at help In the right direction.

tend Await.

bent Arranged.

purposes Dramatic irony. Claudius's real purpose is to dispose of Hamlet, who hints at his suspicion of this in the following line.

mother By equivocating, Hamlet refuses to acknowledge Claudius as his father.

at foot Closely.

leans on Depends on.

England The king of England.

As ... sense Which your experience of my power should make you do.

cicatrice Wound.

free Voluntary.

coldly ... process Treat our royal mandate with indifference.

imports at full Setting out in detail.

congruing to In accordance with.

hectic Fever.

Act IV Scene 4

Fortinbras passes through Denmark on his way to fight the Poles. Hamlet enquires where they are going and, after their departure, compares their fight over a scrap of land with his own failure to act over a truly serious offence.

This scene continues the train of thought in the soliloquy at the end of II,2. The Norwegians have a real but trivial cause, where the Player King had a serious but fictional one.

Commentary

conveyance Safe conduct.

a promis'd march The march agreed upon. See II,2,81.

would aught Wishes to deal.

eye Presence.

softly Carefully.

main Main part.

addition Exaggeration.

farm Rent.

ranker Higher.

in fee Freehold.

debate Settle.

imposthume Swelling.

without Outside.

inform Bring charges.

market Profitable use.

large discourse Wide-ranging reasoning power.

fust Go mouldy.

Of Which results from.

event Consequences. See also l.50 below. This theme is also developed in the soliloquy at III,1,64ff.

mouths Faces.

invisible Unknown.

eggshell i.e. a trivial cause.

Rightly ... stake Hamlet makes a vital discrimination here. True greatness doesn't involve quarrelling over nothing, but over causes which may seem trivial when they represent larger issues of honour – which here means far more than a good name in itself. For more on this see the section on Hamlet's character.

trick Trifle.

Whereon ... cause Which isn't even big enough to provide a site for the battle.

continent Container.

Act IV Scene 5

Ophelia sings and raves, driven mad by the death of her father and the loss of Hamlet's love. The Queen speaks kindly to her and the King pities her condition. When she goes out Laertes enters with a band of followers, intent on revenge for his father's death which he blames on the King. Ophelia re-enters and her brother laments her fate, demanding justice from the King.

This scene develops the parallels and contrasts between the

two families: Laertes' father murdered, like Hamlet's; Ophelia's real madness, unlike Hamlet's; the desire for revenge in both. But Laertes has the support of the mob – a worrying sign for Claudius – and his determination to avenge himself is more urgent than Hamlet's. The King has apparently disposed of Hamlet; now his task is to calm Laertes.

The most touching and pathetic parts of this scene deal with Ophelia, whose madness is nicely timed to coincide with her brother's return. Both of them are disturbed by their father's murder. The Mad Scene is a stock part of seventeenth-century tragedy, and the subject is often a woman, distracted by suffering. The ironic mixture of innocence and obscenity is also typical. It is the combination of her father's death and Hamlet's cruelty which has driven the girl mad, and her madness finds outlet in images of death and sexuality which become entangled in the crazed medley of popular songs and sayings.

Commentary

distract Mad.

Spurns . . . straws Takes angry offence at trifles.

  in doubt Of doubtful meaning.

nothing Meaningless.

collection Collect her remarks, i.e. to make some sort of sense.

  aim Guess.

yield Suggest.

ill-breeding Inclined to think ill.

sin's i.e. the guilt produced by consciousness of sin.

toy Trifle.

  amiss Misfortune.

spills Brings destruction on.

(sings) Ophelia's songs mix reflections on love and death with nonsense and traditional verses. Her father's murder and Hamlet's betrayal are joined in her confused mind.

cockle-hat and staff The marks of a pilgrim.

shoon Shoes.

Larded Decorated.

good dild God reward.

Conceit upon Imaginings about. The King attributes all Ophelia's woe to the loss of her father. (See l.75 below.) The song which follows suggests a different view.

betime Early.

dupp'd Opened. The sexual imagery here is continued throughout the

57

song. It is ironic that such imagery now pervades Ophelia's genuinely mad ramblings as much as it pervaded Hamlet's simulated madness.

Gis A corruption of 'Jesus'.

Cock Corruption of 'God' but with obvious slang reference to the penis.

spies Scouts – the individual soldiers who go before an army reconnoitering.

muddied Muddled – like muddied water.

For About.

hugger-mugger Secret.

Divided from . . . i.e. she is not herself.

fair judgment Reason.

Feeds . . . wonder Broods on this sensation.

in clouds Aloof (though Laertes is about to burst in).

And . . . buzzers And isn't without scandal-mongers. (Note the renewed ear-imagery which follows.)

of matter beggar'd Lacking true facts.

ear and ear Everyone's ears.

murd'ring-piece Cannon scattering shot. Hence 'superfluous'.

Switzers Swiss mercenaries, perhaps more dependable than Danes, under the circumstances.

overpeering of his list Overflowing its bounds.

head Advancing mob.

And, as the world . . . An ironic situation, in view of the way Claudius himself came to the throne.

word Promise (such as their oath of loyalty).

cry i.e. like a pack of hounds on the wrong scent.

this king Observe the contemptuous use of 'this'.

That . . . mother A variation on Hamlet's feelings.

fear Fear for.

divinity Claudius speaks truer than he knows – but the divinity is his brother's, not his.

but peep to Only glance at.

To hell . . . Compare Laertes' abrupt confrontation with Hamlet's approach. Claudius will turn this passion to his own advantage.

grace The grace of God which gives salvation. Even this Laertes will forgo for revenge.

both the worlds Here and in the world to come.

throughly Thoroughly.

stay Prevent.

My . . . world's Only my own will could stop me.

swoopstake Indiscriminately.

pelican Which traditionally fed its young on its own blood.

sensibly Feelingly.

level Clearly.

sense and virtue Perception and power.

turn the beam Tilt the scale.

Nature . . . loves This is obscure. It seems to mean that love refines and sensitizes human nature which then loses something essential in itself to the loved object. In Ophelia's case this may be Hamlet, her father, or both. Having lost them she has therefore lost something vital of herself.

wheel Refrain.

This . . . matter This nonsense says more than sense.

rosemary . . . The plants are appropriate in each case.

A document Instruction.

commune with Share.

collateral Another's.

touch'd Implicated.

hatchment Coat of arms. It isn't clear why Polonius has been buried so unceremoniously.

Act IV Scene 6

A letter is brought to Horatio describing Hamlet's encounter with pirates and his return to Denmark.

Hamlet and Laertes return almost simultaneously. This will suit Claudius very well, if he can match them against one another and ensure that Laertes disposes of Hamlet. He certainly has two good reasons for doing so: Ophelia's madness and his father's death.

Commentary

means Way, introduction.

appointment Equipment.

we . . . valour We engaged them in an inevitable battle.

bore . . . matter Scale of the business. 'Bore' refers to a gun.

way Means. See l.13.

Act IV Scene 7

With some difficulty, the King convinces Laertes of Hamlet's guilt. Laertes is inclined to lay the blame on Claudius and wonders why Hamlet is still free. The King explains that Hamlet is popular; besides, he doesn't want to hurt Gertrude. Encouraging the youth's desire for revenge, Claudius proposes a duel in which Laertes will have an unguarded foil, while the King provides a poisoned chalice to make sure of the job. When the Queen enters with the news of Ophelia's death, Laertes is set on revenge.

The contrast between the hot-blooded Laertes and the intellectual Hamlet is underlined. But so is the contrast between Laertes and the crafty Claudius who intends to use him for his own purposes, to turn the tables on Hamlet. At the end of the play Claudius will neatly succeed in getting one revenger to kill the other — but only at the cost of his own life and Gertrude's. The single moment of honest and balanced feeling in the scene comes in the Queen's tender description of Ophelia's death.

Commentary

seal Confirm.
knowing Understanding.
feats Sinful acts.
capital Punishable by death.
mainly Greatly.
much unsinew'd Very weak.
conjunctive to Closely involved with. The following image comes from astrology.
sphere Course. The Queen is thus the 'course' in which Claudius's star moves.
count Settlement.
general gender Ordinary people.
gyves Fetters, and so the sign of faults.
slightly timber'd Lightly shafted.
go back again Refer to what was.
shook Pulled. A form of insult.
naked Destitute.
kingly eyes ... The letter is couched in ironically obsequious terms.
abuse Trick.
character Handwriting.
devise Explain to.
As how ... otherwise For how should it be done, and how could it be otherwise.
to a peace To make peace.
To ... peace Claudius reassures Laertes that any settlement will be to his satisfaction.
as checking at Having abandoned.
work Manoeuvre.
ripe ... device Mature in my plans.

breathe Blow.

uncharge the practice Not suspect the plot.

The rather All the more.

organ Instrument.

parts Accomplishments.

siege Rank, importance.

A very ribbon A mere decoration.

grew unto Appeared to be one with.

incorps'd and demi-natur'd Of the same body and half the nature.

forgery Simulation. Claudius means he hasn't thoughts (or words) to describe the horseman.

shapes Positions.

made confession Gave an account.

scrimers Fencers.

play Match.

painting . . . Compare I,2,76.

passages of proof Authenticating examples.

qualifies Moderates.

still Permanently.

pleurisy Excess.

That we . . . Claudius takes up Hamlet's theme of 'striking while the iron is hot'.

And . . . easing And then our very consciousness of obligation becomes an excuse for not taking action – which is why it 'hurts by easing'.

quick Tenderest part, i.e. the heart of the matter.

sanctuarize Give protection to.

put on Set to work.

remiss Unsuspecting.

free . . . Claudius is wrong about this.

unbated Not blunted.

Requite Take revenge on.

unction Ointment. 'Unction' and 'anoint' together ironically recall the blessing in church. But Laertes is preparing to send Hamlet to death with all his sins on his head.

  mountebank Quack.

cataplasm Plaster.

simples Medicinal herbs, whose power was enhanced by the influence of the moon.

contagion i.e. the poison.

  gall Scratch.

fit . . . shape Suit our plan.

drift look Plan show.

back or second Fall-back position.

blast in proof Fall apart in practice.

cunnings Skill (of both).

motion Exertion.
nonce Occasion.
stuck Thrust.
askant Aslant.
fantastic Elaborate.
liberal Free-spoken.
  grosser Cruder.
crownet Garlanded.
envious Spiteful.
lauds Songs.
incapable Unaware.
indued ... element Endowed with the ability to live in water.
Till that Before.
lay Song.
trick Way.
the woman ... The feminine element.
this folly douts it The foolishness (of these tears) puts it out.

Revision questions on Act IV

1 In what ways do Laertes and Hamlet resemble their fathers?

2 What is the role of Fortinbras in this act?

3 What is the significance of Ophelia's madness and death?

4 Why does Shakespeare put Laertes at the head of 'the rabble'?

5 What different forms and functions of prose and verse can you identify in this act?

Act V Scene 1

Hamlet and Horatio come upon a grave-digger preparing a grave. Two skulls he turns up lead to Hamlet's reflections on human destiny. A funeral procession arrives with the King, Queen and Laertes, and Hamlet discovers that Ophelia is to be buried. The priest's words suggest that her death was suicide. Laertes, complaining of the meagre rites given to his sister, leaps into the grave for a final farewell. Hamlet joins him there, insisting that his own love for her was far greater, and they fight. They are separated, and Hamlet leaves. The scene ends with Claudius reminding Laertes of their plan.

This scene foreshadows the ending of the play, with the great battle between Laertes and Hamlet, culminating in the deaths of all the remaining major characters. It also changes the mood of the play, Hamlet's reflections on Yorick anticipating his acceptance of fate in the final scene. The comic business of the grave-digger and his friend plays a part here. Before the Court enters and the play returns to blank verse, their dialogue hints at a world outside the claustrophobic confines of the royal family, a world in which death is not the result of sinister plotting but the inevitable end of every life.

Commentary

seeks ... salvation Malaproprism for seeks damnation (by committing suicide): suicides were denied burial in consecrated ground.

crowner Coroner.

sat on her Considered her case.

se offendendo A mistake for *se defendendo* – in self-defence.

wittingly Knowingly. What follows is a parody of legal argument.

argal Therefore, from *ergo* (Latin).

Goodman Delver Master Digger.

quest Inquest.

there thou say'st You are quite right there. The workers reflect on the privileges of their betters.

countenance Permission, i.e. they can get away with it.

even-Christen Fellow Christians.

bore arms ... Gentlemen have a right to coats of arms. Workers live by the strength of their arms. Hence the punning.

unyoke Have done.

mend Increase. The ass is, of course, the other's brain.

Yaughan An unknown reference. Perhaps an inn-keeper.

In youth ... What follows is a muddled version of an actual song.

property of easiness Matter of indifference.

daintier sense Finer sensibility. The point is that repetition dulls us.

intil Into.

such i.e. alive.

That skull ... The skull was a popular topic of commonplace reflections on mortality in the period.

jowls Flings.

Cain's Cain murdered his brother.

politician Intriguer.

o'er-offices Domineers over.

circumvent Outwit.

chopless Jawless.

mazard head. The double moral of these reflections is i) how are the mighty fallen, and ii) all flesh is grass.

revolution i.e. in Fortune's wheel.

and . . . see't If we could but see it.

the breeding To breed.

but . . . with 'em That they are only worth playing skittles with.

quiddities/quillities Quibbles.

statutes . . . recoveries All forms of legal procedure. The strained word-play which follows all points to the morals mentioned above.

box Coffin – but also meaning 'deed-box'.

in that i.e. in parchment. There is no certainty (assurance) of possession in anything, because death comes to us all.

sirrah Form of address to servants.

liest . . . Note the punning here.

quick Living.

absolute Exact.

by the card Precisely – according to the chart.

equivocation will undo us Double meanings will be our downfall. This reflection applies to the court, not the gravedigger, who offers the example of a straightforward man.

three years . . . Allusion unknown.

picked Finicky.

galls his kibe Grazes his chillblain – because even the peasant follows close after the courtier in over-refinement.

ground Reason.

hold Last.

whoreson This is a common oath.

Rhenish Rhine wine.

it i.e. the memory.

gorge rises Stomach churns.

your gibes . . . Compare l.101ff.

on a roar Laughing.

chop-fallen Dispirited. But see note to l.87.

favour Appearance.

Alexander Alexander the Great, a byword for great deeds.

curiously Minutely. Horatio becomes understandably impatient with Hamlet's morbid indulgence.

follow him thither To imagine him thus. 'It' in the next phrase refers to imagination. Hamlet means that it is quite reasonable to reflect on the full possible consequences of death.

Imperious Imperial.

flaw Gust. Hamlet's fanciful rhyme leads neatly back to verse for the Court's arrival.

maimed Diminished.

Fordo Destroy. 'It' because the person is now a thing.

Couch we Let's hide ourselves.

warranty Authority.

order Usual practice. The 'great command' is the King's.

crants Garland. Like the 'strewments' (strewn flowers) these are appropriate to a virgin.

bringing home Funeral service.

sage Solemn.

peace-parted Departed in peace. Note the parallels between this situation and Old Hamlet's.

howling i.e. in Hell.

ingenious sense Vital intelligence.

Pelion According to Greek myth, a mountain piled on another (Ossa) by the Titans in their war with the gods in order to scale Olympus.

Olympus Traditionally the mountain home of the Greek gods. The exaggerated language reflects Laertes' grief, but also leads to the competition at l.264ff.

Conjures Compels.

wonder-wounded Struck with astonishment.

splenative Hot-headed. This is just the outcome Claudius desires.

forbear him Let him be.

'Swounds God's wounds – an oath.

Woo't Would you.

eisel Vinegar. Hamlet's exaggerations seem rather misplaced, now Ophelia is dead, but his point, as usual, is the contrast of mere words with action. He doesn't know that Laertes and Claudius have action of their own in view.

outface me . . . There's more than a hint of self-indulgence here. Laertes didn't even know Hamlet was present. But the two are well-matched.

burning zone The sun's region.

Ossa Ossa was the mountain on which the Titans piled Pelion. See note on l.246 above.

and thou'lt mouth If you'll declaim.

golden couplets Pair of nestlings.

disclos'd Hatched.

the reason . . . Hamlet can hardly fail to understand his opponent's distress, with the prince responsible for a murder and a suicide in his family.

Hercules Proverbially strong Greek hero who was set a number of labours. Even he cannot prevent events taking their course.

patience in Patience by thinking of.

living Lasting. Claudius may be hinting at Hamlet's anticipated death: he is now living but will soon be dead.

Act V Scene 2

Hamlet explains to Horatio how he turned the tables on Rozencrantz and Guildenstern. He decides to make peace with Laertes, but Osric enters to deliver his enemy's challenge. Hamlet accepts the challenge and in so doing consciously accepts his fate, whatever it may be. However, he still offers friendship to Laertes. Laertes responds, but insists on the duel as a matter of honour. Hamlet wins the first two rounds and Gertrude toasts him in the poisoned cup, despite Claudius's warning. In the third round, swords are exchanged and each combatant wounds the other fatally. The Queen dies, Laertes accuses Claudius, who is killed by Hamlet; and Laertes dies after reconciling himself with the prince. Hamlet dies, commending to Denmark Fortinbras, who enters with the English ambassadors. They report the execution of Guildenstern and Rosencrantz in England. The play ends with the ceremonial removal of Hamlet's body.

When Justice has been done, the scene ends in the usual way of Jacobean tragedy with a pile of bodies on stage, but (paradoxically, in view of Hamlet's insistence that actions are more important than words) the carnage is less important than the poetry.

Commentary

this ... i.e. some other matter they have discussed.

circumstance Details.

mutines Mutineers.

bilboes fetters.

Rashly ... What follows is a passage in praise of rashness which shows how far Hamlet has travelled from the deliberations of the 'To be, or not to be' soliloquy.

let us know Note that.

pall Fail.

ends Destinies. Hamlet is preparing to trust himself to fate. It is appropriate that we should learn this while he is relating his adventures, for Shakespeare commonly uses the sea as a symbol of Fortune or Destiny.

sea-gown Sailor's coat or cover.

them This may refer to Rosencrantz and Guildenstern or to their letters.

Finger'd Stole.

in fine At last.

forgetting Overcoming.
Larded Elaborated.
Importing Involving.
bugs ... life Wicked deeds I had been up to.
supervise Reading.
  no leisure bated Without losing a moment.
stay Pause for.
commission Instruction.
Or Before.
  make a prologue Decide what to do.
brains ... In announcing how his mind worked without his volition, Hamlet is clearly describing the moment when the rashness described at l.6ff began to work in him.
fair In good handwriting.
statists Statesmen.
effect Meaning.
conjuration Appeal.
As The first 'As' means 'because', the second and third 'so'.
tributary Payer of tribute.
a comma i.e. something trivial.
shriving-time Time to make confession. Hamlet's letter adopts the same urgent tone as the original.
ordinant In control. The success of this stage of Hamlet's plan gives him confidence to trust in providence for the rest.
that Danish seal The original one broken when Hamlet opened the letter.
subscrib'd Signed.
th'impression i.e. of the seal.
to/ ... sequent Followed.
to't To their death.
near On.
insinuation Interference.
fell ... points Fierce and angry swords.
opposites Opponents.
stand ... upon Now oblige me.
my hopes ... This is the first mention of such hopes.
angle Hook.
  proper Own.
coz'nage Trickery.
perfect In accordance with.
quit Requite, take vengeance on.
canker Disease.
short Very soon.
portraiture Picture. Hamlet now recognizes the similarities.
bravery Extravagance.

water-fly i.e. trifler.

gracious Fortunate.

Let . . . mess If a man is rich you will find him at court.

crib Trough.

mess Table.

chuff Chattering bird.

northerly . . . Compare this passage with III,2,367–73.

complexion Constitution.

for my ease . . . i.e. it is good manners to remove my hat.

absolute Perfect.

differences Distinctions.

soft society Fine manners.

great showing Good appearance.

feelingly Appropriately.

card or calendar Chart and directory. Osric typically uses two words where one will do.

continent . . . see Complement of qualities a gentleman would wish to see.

definement Definition, description. Hamlet replies to Osric in his own language.

perdition Loss.

inventorially In a detailed list.

yaw Diverge (like a ship from its course).

his quick sail i.e. his good qualities.

article Scope.

infusion Quality.

to . . . him To speak truly of him.

semblable Like, i.e. the only person like him.

who else . . . more Whoever would follow him is only his shadow, nothing more. An absurdly roundabout way of saying that there is no one like him.

concernancy Relevance.

more rawer Cruder.

Is't not . . . Horatio wonders at Osric's failure to understand his own diction when another person uses it.

nomination Naming.

approve Recommend.

for his weapon With his sword. Osric refers to specific talents, Hamlet to the man's moral character.

imputation Reputation.

meed Merit.

unfellowed Unmatched.

impawned Wagered.

assigns Fittings.

carriages Straps.

dear to fancy Pleasing to the imagination.

responsive Suited.

liberal conceit Lavish design.

edified Instructed. 'The margin' is where explanatory notes appear.

german Relevant.

a cannon . . . Because a gun rides on a carriage.

French bet . . . Laertes has acquired French ways and equipment.

passes Rounds.

for Instead of.

answer Encounter.

breathing Exercise.

for's turn To do it for him.

This lapwing . . . A proverbial reference to the lapwing's early departure from the nest.

comply with Pay compliments to.

dug Breast.

bevy Flock.

drossy Trivial, frivolous.

tune of the time Fashion of the day.

yeasty collection Frothy prattle.

fanned and winnowed Tried and tested.

blow . . . trial Test them.

are out Collapse.

attend Wait for.

If . . . ready If he is ready, so am I. This means more than it says for both of them.

In happy time At the right moment.

use . . . entertainment Give a courteous welcome.

at the odds i.e. the 'three hits' (cf. l.164).

gaingiving Fearful anticipation.

repair hither Coming here.

in the fall Even in the fall. This refers to Matthew x,29.

If it If death.

betimes Early.

This presence Those who are present.

distraction . . . As we know, Hamlet's madness was feigned; so it's hard to tell whether Hamlet thinks he is telling the truth, making an excuse, or lying. Does he here refer to something other than his antic disposition? A sense that he really was out of his mind in a way he didn't understand? It depends on your interpretation of the play and the character.

exception Disapproval.

If Hamlet . . . Compare IV,5,84. Assuming the reasoning here to be sincere, it is also specious.

purpos'd Intended. This may answer the doubts in the comments above. We can interpret Hamlet as claiming that he didn't kill Polonius or harm Ophelia deliberately because he wasn't acting in his own person – but the case is still weak.

nature Feeling. Contrasted with 'honour' in l.244.

motive Incitement.

and will And will accept.

a voice . . . peace An authority and precedent for making peace.

ungor'd Unstained.

your foil . . . Hamlet uses the word in the other sense: contrast.

stick fiery off Stand out in brilliant contrast.

odds i.e. Hamlet's advantage of three hits.

quit . . . of Come equal in.

better breath Improved skill.

union Pearl.

kettle Kettle-drum.

heaven to earth This recalls earlier cosmic allusions.

this pearl . . . This may be the poison, assuming Claudius only pretends to drink Hamlet's health.

fat Sweaty.

And yet . . . conscience Laertes is having doubts.

make a wanton of Trifle with.

springe Trap.

Unbated Unguarded.

  practice Plot.

union A pun on marriage and the pearl.

temper'd Mixed.

fell Fierce.

unsatisfied Ignorant.

Never believe it i.e. don't imagine I could survive you.

antique Roman i.e. preferring honourable suicide.

Fortinbras . . . Shakespeare is perhaps overdoing things in bringing both the ambassadors and the future king in exactly on cue.

o'ercrows Overpowers.

th'election For the new king.

occurrents Events.

solicited i.e. solicited me to name him king.

quarry Pile of corpses.

  cries on havoc Proclaims slaughter.

toward Imminent.

th'ability of life The ability given by life.

jump Promptly.

  question Matter, affair.

accidental judgments e.g. the death of Polonius.

put on Instigated.

  forc'd Organized.

of memory Remembered.
vantage Opportunity.
his mouth i.e. Hamlet's. His support will encourage others to speak up for Fortinbras.
this same i.e. the funeral rites.
put on Called to the task.
shoot i.e. their cannon.

Revision questions on Act V

1 Explain the importance of the grave-digger's scene. Why does it occur at this point in the play?

2 What part does Osric play in the action?

3 What is the significance of Hamlet's dying reference to Fortinbras?

4 What does Hamlet mean when he speaks of 'special providence' (V,2,215) and what significance do his words have for the play in general?

5 Why does Shakespeare kill Gertrude?

Shakespeare's art in *Hamlet*

Setting

The play is set in Denmark at an unspecified time, but it could be almost anywhere. Shakespeare had little interest in geographical details. Though his tragedies are set in places as far afield as Cyprus and Scotland, particular locales hardly matter. Occasionally places such as Rome and Venice become symbolically significant, but this has more to do with their historical associations than with any physical features. So although *Hamlet* takes place in the castle of Elsinor, it might just as well be Windsor or the Tower of London, there are many references to contemporary English life, not least the inclusion of the travelling players with whom Shakespeare was well acquainted, for obvious reasons.

But if place and time are not important, the political setting of the play is absolutely crucial. The action of *Hamlet* occurs in a characteristic Renaissance court, common in Jacobean drama and instantly recognizable by any member of Shakespeare's audience. The theatrical court derived its features from the Italian city states of the fifteenth century, small places ruled by absolute princes who tyrannized courtiers and populace alike. An atmosphere of terror and intrigue often dominated such cities, which appeared more orderly and gracious than was actually the case. Plots and counter-plots abounded; political assassination was common, even within families or between husbands and wives; and poisoning was a favoured method of murder, made notorious by the Borgias.

The attitude to political life in such places was summed up for the popular imagination by Nicolo Machiavelli's treatise *The Prince* (published in Italy in 1532) which, in the course of describing a good ruler, seems to legitimate every kind of treachery and cynical intrigue among the ruling classes. In fact, Machiavelli is simply pleading for a realistic approach to politics in a country which often verged on anarchy: he suggests that strong government, even if repressive, is preferable to complete chaos. But this was not how many of his readers saw *The Prince* whose methods they equated with the Devil's – hence the name 'Old Nick'.

Claudius's court is a Machiavellian place where plot follows plot and the characters spy on one another. The atmosphere is claustrophobic, tense and degenerate. From the very first scene of the play we are made aware that all is not well in Denmark, and that the trouble comes from the court, though it is left to Hamlet himself to analyse the something that is rotten in the state. In a political system which accumulates all power in the hands of the prince, and all influence in his court, it is inevitable that disorder at the top will create disorder down below. Such disorder flows ultimately from Claudius's initial wicked deed: the murder of his brother. Its effect on Claudius himself is revealed in the prayer-scene (III,3). This effect spreads throughout the state.

An important point here concerns the common view of Shakespeare and Machiavelli: that, had Old Hamlet been a bad king, there might have been some justification for Claudius's deed, though Claudius himself would have suffered all the same, just as Henry IV does when he disposes of Richard II in the history plays. When the ruler is wicked there are grounds for getting rid of him in the larger interests of the state. But Old Hamlet was the very reverse of Claudius. He is constantly praised as the very model of a prince: wise, brave, strong and just. His handsome appearance is the symbol of his political competence. Young Hamlet seems to be his successor in this respect, the paragon of princes referred to by Ophelia (III,1,152ff), though the election ultimately lights on Fortinbras, whom we perceive as the true successor to Old Hamlet. So the setting of the play is the occasion for another episode in Shakespeare's long-running meditation on the nature of power and the character of the good ruler, which are common themes of sixteenth- and seventeenth-century literature.

Structure

The structure of the play is determined by Hamlet's need to avenge the murder of his father by his uncle. Hamlet and Claudius are therefore the two pivots about whom the play turns, and the structure arises from their plots against one another. On the one hand Hamlet seeks vengeance, on the other Claudius seeks to eliminate him. This produces a series of strikes and counterstrikes along the following lines:

(a) Claudius plots successfully to seize the throne and his brother's wife.

(b) Urged on by the Ghost, Hamlet stages *The Mousetrap* to trap his uncle while feigning madness to protect himself.

(c) Claudius then plots against Hamlet by exiling him to England with instructions for his death. Polonius is in the exile plot but not in the death-plot.

(d) Hamlet foils this plot and returns to deal with Claudius, though he doesn't yet know how.

(e) Claudius plots with Laertes against Hamlet. They will stage a rigged duel and Claudius will poison Hamlet's drink.

(f) Claudius's plot succeeds – but rebounds against him when (i) Gertrude drinks the poison, and (ii) Laertes reveals the plot.

So Claudius engineers his own death – but so does Hamlet. The symmetry is complete. The entire royal family (and their closest advisers) are wiped out, and the dynasty begins again with Fortinbras.

This basic plot-structure is complicated and refined by many other elements in the play: the tangle of relationships, the use of foils (such as Horatio), the political background. But in the end everything boils down to the struggle between Claudius and Hamlet. The balance of dramatic interest is tilted in Hamlet's favour not only because of Claudius's wicked deeds, but because Hamlet is developed in such detail and in ways which engage audience sympathy. To understand this we might compare the play with *Macbeth*. In that drama the central figure is himself a kind of Claudius. Macbeth and his wife murder the rightful king and seize the throne, but their usurpation is later avenged and they are destroyed. Had Shakespeare called his play *Claudius* and emphasized the king's part at the expense of Hamlet's (relegating him to Fortinbras's role at the end of the play) things would look very different. We can see how he might have done this from the prayer-scene in which Claudius unsuccessfully attempts to express true penitence. In the event, Shakespeare dwells on the character of Hamlet, restoring the balance by making the king the main initiator of events. The relationship between these two very different figures is therefore absolutely crucial to the play's structure at every level: dramatically, thematically, morally, emotionally.

Revenge tragedy and *Hamlet*

Revenge tragedy was popular in the sixteenth and seventeenth centuries. *Hamlet*, and Webster's play *The Duchess of Malfi*, in which the character Bosola bears some resemblance to the Danish prince, are perhaps the most famous examples; but there are earlier plays in this genre which probably influenced Shakespeare, including *The Spanish Tragedy* and *The Revenger's Tragedy*. Such plays have many similar features besides the theme of revenge. Ghosts are common, violent death is the usual outcome for most of the characters, and spectacle is an important part of the action. Justice is brutally meted out, to the accompaniment of a moralizing text, made more palatable in Shakespeare and Webster by the brilliant imagery of the speeches, and the subtle development of the major characters.

The theme of revenge derives ultimately from Greek tragedy in which it is part of a complex debate about the nature of justice. Like *Hamlet*, these ancient plays are about blood feuds between and within families. One very remote model for the hero of Shakespeare's play is Orestes, the man who kills his mother and her lover in order to avenge their murder of his father. Shakespeare knew something of the saga from which this story comes in the versions made by Roman poets and playwrights, including Seneca, whose versions of Greek tragedies had a powerful influence on sixteenth-century drama. Seneca stressed the violent, bloody and horrific elements in his sources – as we can see from *Titus Andronicus*, the Shakespeare play which manifests his influence most clearly. His plays are like modern horror stories in which the philosophical context of the Greek tragedies has given way to sensationalism.

But Greek drama constantly invokes the gods: revengers such as Orestes are seen to be justified only in so far as they embody divine justice. Even then, they may be punished on account of their impious deeds, for the ironic essence of revenge tragedy is that the tragic hero cannot escape wreaking one wrong in order to avenge another. This is precisely Hamlet's predicament: he must commit a sin (murder) in order to punish the same offence in someone else. Hamlet is therefore only ready to kill Claudius when he accepts his destiny as an instrument of the divine will. His success brings about his own death. He is punished for doing what he must do.

Themes

It isn't possible or desirable to single out any one theme in the play. Complex works of art range over many themes, and where plays are concerned, much can depend on the way in which they are performed. In addition, the richness of Shakespeare's imagery and the allusiveness of his language weave the themes together in an elaborate tapestry. All we can do is to pull out some of the threads in this tapestry in order to examine the thematic web. In a writer like Shakespeare the thematic and metaphoric elements of his work cannot finally be prized apart.

Two main groups of themes emerge from the play with special force. The first group involves personal, political, judicial and even cosmic relationships. The second involves Shakespeare's familiar obsession with appearance and reality.

Relationships

Revenge

Holding the whole play together is the theme of revenge. This generates the plot and permeates Hamlet's soliloquies. As the play progresses we perceive that revenge is not, of itself, a legitimate objective, but justified only in so far as it is a form of divine justice. By the same token, the revenger must be an agent of that justice, and not in the business of settling scores. What legitimizes Hamlet's pursuit of Claudius is that there is more here than a personal grievance. Claudius is certainly responsible for the crime of killing Hamlet's father, for which he deserves punishment – but the fact that Hamlet's father was a king is no accidental circumstance. Claudius has disturbed the order of nature, hence Hamlet's frequent appeals to Heaven and Earth. As both the victim's son and a possible heir to the throne, his nephew is therefore the appropriate agent of providence, but he can only become so when he has learnt to distance himself from vindictiveness.

As the previous paragraph suggests, the theme of revenge is closely bound up with two other sets of themes common in

Shakespeare, concerning the nature of order and the meaning of providence.

Order

In Shakespeare's universe both the human order and the divine are hierarchical, with the king or God at the top and the other creatures ranged below. The first is an image of the second. But there is also a tendency in Nature to disorder, which occurs in men when their baser urges take control, as they have in Claudius. Because man is part god and part beast, as Hamlet points out, the divinity of his reason (the source and guarantee of order) is often likely to be tainted or undermined by the drives of his beast-nature. If this should happen to the monarch, his disorder infects the whole of society, as must be inevitable in an hierarchical system. The revenger's higher purpose, therefore, is not merely to punish wickedness, but to restore order. Images of the sick body and the unweeded garden are constantly cited in the play to make this point: the revenger is to the state as the doctor to the body and the gardener to the garden, a rational intelligence adjusting unregenerate nature.

Providence

Such agents of order are also therefore the agents of providence, for it is assumed that the universe tends to order under the guidance of a benevolent creator, and that disorder is an aberration from the higher truth of existence. The play makes this point in several ways, mainly by showing the unpleasant consequences which ensue from the breakdown of order. The cause of the breakdown in *Hamlet* is Claudius's murder of his brother and seizure of his throne and wife. This is an offence against the natural order in several ways: as murder, as fratricide, as usurpation, and as incest. He is therefore guilty on four major counts.

Monarchy

His guilt suggests the importance of a fourth theme connected with the others: the nature of monarchy and the good ruler. This is a theme Shakespeare explores in the history plays and in the other tragedies. If the monarch's behaviour affects the whole of society, it is clearly crucial – and Shakespeare is careful to tell us what an exemplary figure Hamlet's father was in this respect. His handsome and noble appearance, often referred to, are outward signs of his fitness to rule – just as Claudius's inferiority is a sign of the opposite. This is true even though Claudius has managed to conceal his crime: the insistent imagery of inward decay, and the Ghost's revelation to Hamlet, are accompanied by the general sense that there is, in the famous phrase, 'something rotten in the state of Denmark'. The word 'state' here refers both to the place and the political condition of the country; and the source of the rot is Claudius himself, though only Hamlet and the Ghost know the full truth.

The good king is one who respects the laws of providence. No one who seizes the throne by force from its rightful occupant can succeed in the end, however talented a ruler. Hence the importance of Hamlet's endorsement of Fortinbras at the very end of the play. All lawful authority has broken down, but with his dying words the prince gives his sanction to a new order. There is then no need for Fortinbras to seize the throne: he can take it as rightfully his. And the peripheral part of Fortinbras suggests a further, subordinate theme: the character and education of a prince. Four young men are introduced into the play: Hamlet, Fortinbras, Horatio and Laertes. Of the four, only the first two have the upbringing, education and character to rule, and we are often told what a paragon Hamlet is in this respect. But fate is against him – and that leaves only Fortinbras, whose courage and sense of honour (see IV,4) fit him for the throne.

Politics

Linked with the theme of monarchy is the theme of politics in general. So much attention has been paid to the character of Hamlet that we are apt to forget this. But the play is as much about power as it is about the inner suffering of the protagonist. The tragedy takes place at court, where Claudius and Hamlet are involved in a life-and-death struggle: that is the core of the play. The struggle is made necessary by the fact that Claudius has already successfully plotted to overthrow his brother. One plot leads to another, as Hamlet and his uncle plan and counter-plan. Shakespeare's contemporaries were fascinated by the spectacle of political power, and in particular by the mixture of intrigue and savage violence it seemed to involve.

But Hamlet and his uncle are not alone. All the other major characters are involved in the power-play one way or another. Polonius is a parody of the stereotypical councillor, foolish and long-winded by turns, fond of strategems, and fatally trusting in his own powers of perception and judgement. Laertes briefly becomes Claudius's tool, to the misfortune of both. Horatio is Hamlet's trusted adviser. Ophelia and Gertrude are swept along in the dangerous train of plots made by their male relations.

Meanwhile, a vivid background to the fate of the royal family and their closest associates is provided by the murmurings of the mob. Mentioned several times, this finally erupts into the play in Act IV, scene 5, when Laertes returns from Paris to claim justice. We are thus reminded how precarious is the situation of even the most powerful ruler. The sixteenth century was a hierarchical age in which the king officially derived his right to rule from God, the nobility took their lands and privileges at the pleasure of the king, and so on down the line to the peasants who worked the land. Concentrating all power in the king's hands, this system needed a strong and wise ruler to make it work. Signs of weakness or abuse could easily precipitate popular disorder, as in *Hamlet*. By murdering the previous king, Claudius has disturbed the very hierarchy from which he claims to derive his own power. His downfall is the just consequence of this act. At the end of the play Fortinbras appears as the strong, just ruler who can restore social harmony, and become the true 'father' to his subjects Claudius can never be – any more than he can be a true father to Hamlet himself.

Parents and children

If the relationship between the ruler and his subjects is shaped by an hierarchical sense of order, so is the relationship between parents and children, which leads us to another theme of the play. There are two sets of parents and children in *Hamlet*: the prince, his mother, father and stepfather; Laertes, Ophelia and Polonius. Early on in the play these relationships are emphasized, first by the powerful contrast between Hamlet's attitude to his stepfather and his encounter with the Ghost, then in the scene of Laertes' departure for Paris and Polonius's interview with Ophelia. In I,2 Shakespeare draws our attention to the apparent difference between Laertes' submissiveness to Polonius and Hamlet's rudeness to Claudius – but we soon become aware that Hamlet is all obedience to his real father, whereas Laertes is a considerable hothead.

The theme is perhaps most powerfully brought out when Hamlet reproaches his mother (III,4) with the spectral presence of Old Hamlet in the background. The young prince is torn between love and disgust, pity and duty. He owes obedience to his mother, as to his father, but she has fallen short of her duty, thereby forfeiting the privilege of her place in the natural order. Obedience to his father therefore takes precedence.

Appearance and reality

Just as the theme of revenge holds the whole play together, so the theme of appearance and reality pervades everything in it. Some of the ways in which it does this are obvious. Hamlet's feigned madness, for example, confuses the other characters, as he means it to do: they cannot tell whether he is really mad or just behaving eccentrically. Nor are they certain of the source of this madness, if madness it be.

Take also the case of Claudius. He appears to be the legitimate king of Denmark. No one challenges his right to the throne, not even Hamlet. But we know that he is not the legitimate king, that he took the throne by force, and that he has deceived even his brother's wife. And as Hamlet points out, Claudius is her true husband only in appearance: her real loyalty should be to Old Hamlet.

Then again, Claudius appears to be confidently in control. But in the prayer scene (III,3) we discover that this is far from the case: that Claudius is wracked with guilt and uncertainty. This scene is an especially complex and ironic example of the appearance/reality theme. After Hamlet's decision not to kill the king because he is at prayer, we discover that he only appeared to be praying: his inability to give up the spoils of his sin renders his prayers null and void. And when Hamlet reflects on his delay, we begin to wonder whether he only appears to want to kill Claudius – just as, earlier, he himself has wondered whether the Ghost is just a deceitful apparition sent from Hell, not really the spirit of his father at all.

The appearance/reality dichotomy also manifests itself in the way the characters watch one another to divine the truth behind their public behaviour. At the beginning of the play Claudius and Gertrude criticize Hamlet's show of grief, and he angrily insists that it has a reality beyond mere show. A little later Polonius spies on Hamlet with Ophelia, and then with his mother. Hamlet watches the king during the performance of The Mousetrap to see if he will give himself away, and encourages Horatio to do the same. Francisco and Barnardo watch for the Ghost, wondering whether it is real. Hamlet spies on the King at his prayers. The Ghost watches over Hamlet and Gertrude. Rosencrantz and Guildenstern are sent to spy on Hamlet – and Hamlet spies on them when he opens the letters they are carrying from Claudius. Hamlet criticizes women for their preoccupation with show.

Once again, the play within the play is central to the working out of this theme: it is something Claudius *watches* which gives him away – but the play means one thing to him (and to Hamlet), another to the rest of the court.

Closely connected with this constant watching is the theme of truth and falsehood. Claudius's whole life is now based on a lie, as well as a murder. Gertrude, too, has deceived herself, as she realizes when Hamlet confronts her with the facts of the case (III,4). The play is full of deception. Hamlet pretends to be mad. Polonius makes his daughter draw Hamlet into conversation and instructs Reynaldo to lie in the service of his son (II,1). The King sends secret letters to England with Rosencrantz and Guildenstern, and Hamlet turns the same letters against them. The King and Laertes plot against Hamlet. Gertrude agrees to lie on Hamlet's behalf (III,4,199).

Philosophy

Dividing the play into themes is just a way of talking about it. The same can be said of imagery. It would be foolish to suppose that Shakespeare himself was aware of the text in this way. Indeed, the evidence suggests that, in contrast with self-conscious writers like Webster, Shakespeare paid the minimum of attention to such matters.

However, underpinning the themes and images there are certain philosophical preoccupations which, though historically commonplace, show signs of elaborate and careful working in the play. The first of these concerns human nature. Broadly speaking, Renaissance writers took the view that Man appears on the scale of creation half-way between angels and beasts. Like angels he has a soul, like beasts a body – and uniquely (as Hamlet points out at II,2,305) the faculty of reason. But the idea is given a new twist in this play because the angel and the beast in man have fallen apart, in the persons of Old Hamlet and his brother Claudius. Hence Hamlet's disgust with the physical (and especially sexual world) which is Claudius's, and his fascination with the world of ideals associated with his father.

If Man is half-way up the hierarchy of creation, he also has his own hierarchy with kings at the top and everyone else below. This social and political order is a reflection of the divine order of the cosmos and nature. It is a common assumption in Shakespeare and his contemporaries that disturbance in one creates disturbance in the other. Trouble on earth is displeasing to heaven. This point is made at the very beginning of the play when Horatio describes the horrors which portended the fall of Julius Caesar (I,1,115ff). These lines are recalled in the closing moments of the play, again by Horatio who speaks 'Of carnal, bloody, and unnatural acts' (V,2,386). In between these two moments frequent allusion is made to the pairing of heaven and earth, the cosmic and the natural order.

Although kings are at the political summit of the human hierarchy, they are not necessarily the most highly developed men. Hamlet, for example, is a far more distinguished character than Claudius. Accordingly he is cited (by both Ophelia and Horatio) as the standard of what a human being might be. The Renaissance ideal of humanity was essentially aristocratic. A superior man was one who easily combined both the military and intellectual qualities of the courtier: courage, wit, grace, beauty – and above all, honour.

Honour is not easy to define in this context. It is subtler than pride or rectitude, though it includes both. Hamlet reflects on it most explicitly in Act IV, scene 4 when he considers the expedition of Fortinbras and his men to Poland to fight for a scrap of land. What Hamlet admires here is not the exploit itself but the spirit which produces it. This is the spirit of honour and it is what makes life worth living at a higher level than the beasts. His revenge therefore becomes a point of honour, not because it is a blood-feud as in so many revenge tragedies, but because he sees that not to pursue it would be implicitly to declare his father's life and all that it stood for worthless – and to admit the victory of the bestial Claudius.

In this context it is worth remarking how little religious feeling there is in this play (and elsewhere in Shakespeare), though religion is used for dramatic effects, as in the prayer scene. There is a metaphysical scheme in the play in the sense that Hamlet and the other characters have a sense of other-worldly realities (embodied primarily in the Ghost) but this 'other' world is not the object of their rapt attention, as it might be in such writers as Donne or Milton, merely the source of ultimate justice. For all the Ghost's supernatural promptings, what matters in *Hamlet* is the human world.

Style

Verse, prose and songs

All Shakespeare's plays use a mixture of prose and verse for reasons which aren't easy to specify. Some of the prose passages in this play are just as lyrical as the verse; while much of the verse is as knotty and colloquial as prose. But prose is often preferred for broad comedy. The exchanges between Polonius, Hamlet and the Players (II,2), Hamlet's encounter with Osric (V,2), and the Grave-digger's scene (V,1), are all largely in prose, though the text moves easily from prose to verse and back, which can be hard to detect in performance.

Within the prose medium different styles are discernible. The earthy, colloquial humour of the Grave-digger's scene is a world away from Osric's foppish elaborations, which are closer to Polonius's absurd verbosities. Both Osric and Polonius are parodies of court life, their elaborate similes and periphrases exaggerated versions of the polite and formal language prescribed for courtiers in the etiquette manuals of the period.

Different again is the prose of Hamlet's speeches in II,2, which contrasts with the pompous verses spoken by the actors. At such moments Shakespeare seems to relish his own facility and ability to distance himself from the medium which was his own starting-point as a dramatist (as we can see if we look at his early plays).

Hamlet more commonly speaks in blank verse, the play's dominant mode, as it is in all Shakespeare's other dramatic works. This verse is occasionally punctuated by rhyming couplets, usually at the end of scenes or speeches when they are employed to make a point. And within the verse, as within the prose, differences of style are made. Compare, for example, the lyrical beauty of the Queen's elegy for Ophelia (IV,7,165ff) with Polonius's absurd pontificating (II,2,85ff); or the formality of Claudius's first speech (I,2,1ff) with Hamlet's passionate intensity at I,2,129ff.

Typical of the theatre in this period is the frequent interpolation of isolated stanzas into the regular texture of the play. These are often taken from popular songs or old ballads and chosen for contemporary allusions since lost; but at certain moments their power is undiminished, and nowhere more so than in Ophelia's mad scene (IV,5).

The Mad Scene was a standard fixture of tragic drama and remained so well into the nineteenth century, finding renewed vigour in romantic opera where the old songs formed part of the musical score. Such an episode gave actresses and singers a chance to show off their histrionic powers as well as providing dramatic and pathetic moments in the drama. Some writers dragged in such scenes for sensational effect, even when they weren't strictly necessary. Shakespeare is careful to work his mad scene into the logical development of the action, but in other respects it is conventional in form if superior to many examples. The quotations and allusions are appropriate (see Commentary), but what really matters is the opportunity for the actress to sing before her death, like Desdemona in *Othello*. The audience's emotions are thus sensitized by this lyrical interlude before the play's final burst of action.

Soliloquies

The most important verse in *Hamlet*, however, is not to be found in the songs but in the protagonist's soliloquies, which are perhaps the most famous in dramatic literature, and with good reason. They are both great set pieces, like arias in an opera, and integral parts of the developing drama. They are also one of the severest tests for any actor, both in shaping individual speeches, and in relating them to the play as a whole; and many performers have testified to the exhausting demands the play makes on the hero.

The purpose of a soliloquy is to take us into the character's private world, and to reveal to the audience what he might not reveal to any other character. It therefore establishes a special link between audience and actor, which is a powerful weapon in engaging audience sympathy. This is true even when the speaker is a figure such as the evil Iago in *Othello*. In that play Shakespeare makes brilliant use of the villain's soliloquies to overcome what might otherwise be our unthinking hatred. Instead of simply hissing at Iago, we learn to see him as a complex, ironic, tortured human being – and this response produces an immeasurable enhancement of the play's depth and power.

In *Hamlet*, the villain has only one soliloquy (III,3) but it provides a crucial moment in which our sympathies are engaged with Claudius while he wrestles with his conscience – not to speak of the exquisite irony by which Hamlet mistakes his sterile prayers for the real thing and so refrains from killing him. Claudius's soliloquy is a perfect example of the technique's potential for altering our view of a situation. Up to that scene the King is merely the urbane ruler or the villainous usurper – a two-dimensional figure, either way. After that scene we can view him as a full participant in the drama. This is an important point when we remember that the plot hinges on the struggle between Hamlet and his uncle. If Claudius were to remain a cardboard character, the struggle would be too unevenly balanced and the play that much diminished in force. (For more on this see the section on Claudius's character.)

Claudius's soliloquy has a double role to fulfil, in that it is overheard by the audience and witnessed (but *not* heard) by Hamlet. This is multiply ironic in a play which makes such a feature of eavesdropping, because it is what he doesn't hear that makes Hamlet decide not to kill Claudius when he could.

The prince's own soliloquies all take place in private. For all Polonius's plots, nothing is overheard*, except by the audience – but what they hear is crucial to their interpretation of the play. Indeed, most accounts of *Hamlet* depend heavily on the interpreter's understanding of the soliloquies which form an accompaniment to the action of the play, and have often been used to explain that action. For it is in the soliloquies that Hamlet seems to reveal his notorious indecisiveness, frequently reproaching himself for failing to act promptly.

A word of warning is in order here. Nothing in a Shakespeare play should ever be taken entirely literally. It may well be that Hamlet does delay a little, though it must be said on the other hand that opportunities for murder are not always easily found. But we must also remember that what the soliloquies reveal is not the facts of the case but also how Hamlet feels about them. Furthermore, the soliloquies are part of the playwright's overall dramatic strategy: they serve to engage the audience's interest and focus their attention on Hamlet, while providing moments of reflection on the action of the play. They thus have a double

*Except possibly 'To be, or not to be . . .' Critics are divided over this.

function, illuminating the character's sense of his predicament while opening up wider perspectives. Shakespeare's great plays constantly hover between the dramatic, the lyrical, and the philosophical: a soliloquy is the point at which all three tendencies meet. (For an account of the soliloquies in sequence see the section on Hamlet's character.)

Imagery

An important aspect of the soliloquies is their imagery. As usual in Shakespeare, certain images are recurrent in the play, and this helps to knit the soliloquies into the text. But each soliloquy also has its own vivid touches. Take the first, in Act I, scene 2. After his opening address, Hamlet introduces the notion of the overgrown garden (I,2,135) which is to be found again and again in the play, sometimes associated with the general state of Denmark, sometimes with the emotions or desires of this or that character. Here it is applied to the whole world, which is Hamlet's hyperbolic way of describing his grief. But the notion of a garden dominated by 'things rank and gross in nature' also points forward to his view of Gertrude's love for Claudius, which is really the source of his disgust. It is hinted that desire grows like a poisonous weed, choking the tenderer plants of love and virtue.

From the garden Hamlet moves on to a comparison between his father and uncle on the one hand, the sun-god and a satyr on the other (l.140). This suggests another train of allusions in the play, which constantly praises Old Hamlet at his brother's expense, emphasizing the natural difference between different sorts of men, even between brothers. This in turn hints at another theme, concerning the appropriate qualities for a king.

But Hamlet's admiration for his father is intimately connected in his mind with his father's virtuous love for Gertrude, which might resemble the relationship of heaven and earth (l.141), unlike the incestuous passion of Claudius. It is, of course, just the right relation between heaven and earth, between the will of God and its execution in this world, which Claudius has disturbed by slaying his brother and incestuously marrying the brother's widow. So the references to heaven and earth, taken up elsewhere in the play, have another function, suggesting the disorder which has overtaken Hamlet's life. Such disorder is embodied in the bestial marriage of Gertrude and Claudius (l.150) which brings in yet another theme: the double nature of Man, at once animal and spiritual.

All these images recur throughout the play. In among them, there is one exquisite, vivid touch peculiar to this speech, which gives Hamlet's general reflections a solidity and immediacy which might otherwise be lacking. At l.147 he refers to:

A little month, or ere those shoes were old
With which she follow'd my poor father's body

The shoes make his point better than any amount of ranting against his mother, by persuading us that Hamlet has a real grievance, not a self-indulgent moan. Gertrude has cast off her last husband as she might cast off an old shoe: the image's incongruity suggests both her shallowness and Hamlet's shock.

Disease

The play's images are complex and varied but two strands stand out: the imagery of disease and corruption, and the imagery of appearance and reality. These two strands correspond to two major themes (see *Themes*).

The imagery of disease is inaugurated in the very first lines of the play with Francisco's statement that he is 'sick at heart' (I,1,9). 'At heart' can mean either 'in my feelings' or 'at my core' and the ambiguity is prophetic. For not only is the whole state of Denmark seen to be sickly: its sickness originates from within its heart, i.e. from the King. This gives rise to a whole series of metaphors depending on abscesses, internal diseases, and inward rottenness. Hamlet describes his mother's incest as an 'ulcerous place' and a 'blister' which infects all around it (III,4). The war between Norway and Denmark is called a tumour. 'Sickly day', 'foul disease', and 'pleurisy' are all terms applied to Claudius. Hamlet sees the sky as nothing but a 'foul and pestilent congregation of vapours' (II,2). Laertes refers to Hamlet's love for Ophelia as a 'canker' (I,3).

Closely associated with images of diseases are the references to dirt and corruption which colour the play, especially where Hamlet's attitudes to love and sex are concerned. His horror at Gertrude's incest is vividly conveyed in lines which describe

the rank sweat of an enseamed bed,
Stew'd in corruption . . . (III,4,92–3)

and both the imagery and the tone of these lines are pursued throughout the scene, as they are in his bitter exchanges with Ophelia, when he attributes to her what he sees as his mother's lecherous desires. Hamlet here takes a line from the Ghost who refers to the lust which will 'prey on garbage' (I,4,57). The poisoning of the old king itself becomes a part of the imagery of corruption in a complex web of allusions which link the poisoning of the body, the state, marriage, and the mind.

Also linked with the imagery of dirt and disease is the imagery of the unweeded garden. The garden has always been potent as a symbol of the order which can be discovered in nature. Such order requires careful tending: if the garden is neglected or abused, disorder soon takes its place. Weeds are to the garden what disease is to the body and injustice to the state: a troublesome interference with its proper working which can prove fatal if allowed to get out of hand. In *Hamlet* this image appears negatively for the most part, in references to the rank growth of weeds. Claudius himself is a kind of weed which flourishes in the untended garden of Denmark.

Appearance and reality

The ironic and even tragic difference between what is the case and what appears to be, is a commonplace of literature in the seventeenth century. In Shakespeare's work it is intimately connected with the playwright's understandable interest in dramatic pretence. Hence the preoccupation in this play with acting.

At the heart of the drama is the play within the play. It is this enactment of Claudius's crime which convinces Hamlet of his uncle's guilt and strengthens his resolve to seek revenge. Before the performance takes place Hamlet reflects in a soliloquy on the difference between the Player-king's cause for passion and his own, the one fictional, the other real (II,2,544ff). These reflections are complicated for the audience by the fact that Hamlet's cause is as fictional as the Player-king's – yet also by the curious way in which our sense of Hamlet's 'reality' is strengthened by the artificiality of the actor's performance.

The comparison of different orders of illusion here is not by the way in *Hamlet*, which often invites us to ponder the question of what is real, what false. The Ghost is one of these elements, Hamlet's feigned madness another. Though some commentators have tried to explain the ghost as a projection of Hamlet's imagination or even a collective hallucination, this goes clean against all the evidence in the play. The Ghost is seen by different people at different times, including Hamlet's sceptical friend Horatio. Hamlet's madness is a 'performance' analogous to the Player-king's: a stratagem for defeating Claudius, but also an illusion inviting the king to betray himself. In the original of the Hamlet story, the hero feigns simple-mindedness to persuade the king that he is no danger, but in *Hamlet* the phenomenon is more complex. Because clear motivation is not provided our attention is diverted to the phenomenon itself, and its effects on Claudius, Polonius and Ophelia. It provides Hamlet with a mask behind which he can hide, and an excuse for his erratic behaviour. More subtly, it suggests his own uncertainty about himself. If the Ghost provides him with a motive for action, the madness allows him leisure to reflect on that action.

The characters

Hamlet and characterization

Before discussing the characters a word of warning is in order. *Hamlet* is a play, not a novel, and the two forms do not work in the same way. This obvious point is often overlooked. Traditional novels tend to focus on character, often in very great detail. Drama is primarily concerned with action. Of course the two cannot be separated: character gives rise to action, which in turn moulds character. But if we ignore the different emphasis in each and treat a play like a novel, as the great nineteenth-century critics were inclined to do, it can obscure the vital difference.

Hamlet

Hamlet is especially prone to this treatment because audiences have been so entranced by the protagonist. In consequence, critics focus on his character when discussing the play. This approach produces a number of unnecessary problems.

Take for example the question which has been so hotly debated for over two hundred years: why does Hamlet delay his revenge when he has the opportunity to take it? Most of the answers to this question are couched in terms of Hamlet's character. Hazlitt, for example, suggests that Hamlet procrastinates because he is a sensitive soul, capable of acting only on impulse, but otherwise paralysed by reflection. Hazlitt's contemporary, Coleridge, put forward a similar explanation. According to him, Hamlet knows what he must do and is resolved to do it, but lacks the resolution to carry out his purpose, largely because his inner life is so much more important to him than anything which happens in the outside world.

These are both interesting and suggestive accounts of the play based on textual evidence. Hamlet does indeed reproach himself for being slow to act (see e.g. II,2,56off) and the sheer length of the play suggests a certain reluctance on his part. But such attempts to make sense of things in terms of Hamlet's character lead both critics to ignore equally strong arguments on the other side. As Bradley points out, there is no evidence whatever in the play to suggest that Hamlet is dilatory by nature. On the contrary: we deduce from Ophelia's description of him as the observed of all observers (III,1,157) that Hamlet is the very model of an active prince, not only a scholar but also a soldier.

It is perhaps significant that both Coleridge and Hazlitt comment on the way in which all readers and spectators find something of themselves in Hamlet. It is this fact, they think, which explains his universal popularity. So we aren't surprised when Coleridge's Hamlet sounds very like Coleridge himself: clever, subtle, imaginative, and full of great schemes which he is incapable of putting into effect. The Romantic poets were inclined to find in Hamlet a man of their own sort, and their interpretations have remained popular.

Some of their successors, especially among German philosophers, have taken this process even further, writing of the play as though it were a poem, with Hamlet as the author, the other characters products of his imagination, This is an intriguing idea, but it doesn't help us to understand *Hamlet* as a play, i.e. the working out of conflict in action. The fact that some of this action is internal, taking place within Hamlet's consciousness, makes no difference to this basic principle: the character is part of the play, not vice versa. To understand the character, we must understand the play.

My intention is not to suggest that Hamlet has no poetic or philosophical qualities: of course he does, and they become apparent as he reflects eloquently upon his predicament. Nor do I want to claim that we should not think of him as a fully-fledged character, when we cannot do otherwise. But Hamlet is not a philosopher or a poet. He doesn't delay because of a constitutional inability to act, or a paralysing melancholy. He is presented as a prince at a rough-and-ready northern court placed in a painful situation and challenged in the most extraordinary way to exact revenge for his father's death. Whatever symbolic interpretations we may attach to the play, these dramatic facts should not slide out of view.

The first we hear of the prince is Horatio's resolve to tell him about the Ghost's appearance (I,1,170). The long and complex account of Denmark's political and military condition in the opening scene prefaces the announcement that the Ghost will speak to him but to no one else – a clear indication that the information we've been given is only background to the crucial event: Young Hamlet's encounter with his dead father. It is this encounter which sets the action in motion.

The following scene delays the prince's début still further, though his ostentatiously black costume and melancholy manner, in sharp contrast with the rest of the Court, draw our attention to him. He appears on stage but does not speak until l.64, after Claudius has addressed the court, the ambassadors to Norway, Laertes and Polonius. When Hamlet finally speaks, his first words are an aside, followed by a wrangle with the King and Queen about what they regard as his excessive grief. It is only when the stage clears at l.129 that the audience has its first direct encounter with Hamlet.

Such apparently cumbersome preliminaries all lead up to the first soliloquy, which reflects with disgust on the scene we have just witnessed, i.e. the happy union of Hamlet's mother and uncle. Our first introduction to Hamlet is therefore as someone who stands apart from ordinary life by virtue of his misfortune and his grief – and at this stage of the play we may well agree with Claudius and Gertrude that he is indulging his emotions. The old king has been dead for almost two months: we might at least expect the young prince to keep his grief to himself now. The fact that he does not, introduces us to two dramatically important aspects of his character: i) his deeply-felt emotions, and ii) his theatrical disposition.

Both these aspects are embodied in his behaviour and alluded to in the imagery of his speeches, which make ironic play with the difference between reality and appearance. His lines at I,2,76ff are especially significant here. Hamlet specifically disclaims the mere appearance of grief in favour of the reality – yet these very lines and the mood which produces them are evidence that he is more concerned with appearance than he likes to admit. If he were really indifferent to appearances, he would oblige his mother with smiles while keeping grief alive secretly in his heart. The depth of his feeling becomes apparent at I,2,129ff, where he reveals his own at the hasty remarriage of his mother to a man who is so far inferior to her first husband.

What the first scene makes clear is that, while Hamlet reveals his true thoughts and feelings when alone or with the Ghost, in public and with others there is frequently a contradiction between what he says and what he does. This contradiction is made explicit in his assumption of the 'antic disposition' and in the verbal fencing with Polonius, Rosencrantz and Guildenstern. And even in the passionate scene with his mother, while the Ghost hovers by, he is bitterly ironic (III,4). Such equivocation is appropriate for a play in which nothing is ever quite what it seems or is said to be, and it is only dispelled at the very end of the play with the death of all the major characters.

In I,5 Hamlet is shaken out of his grief-stricken state by the Ghost's revelation and resolves to begin on a course of action which will lead to revenge. The first step is his assumption of the 'antic disposition' – which seems to be in place by the time he visits Ophelia (II,1,77ff). She describes him as acting out the very picture of grief he disdains at I,2,76ff. Having rejected mere appearances, he has now learnt how to use them for his own ends. The deception is kept up with Polonius (II,2,170ff), continued in a minor key with Rosencrantz and Guildenstern – and then appropriately abandoned when the real Players arrive and Hamlet reverts to his ordinary self.

Act II finishes with the famous soliloquy beginning 'O what a rogue and peasant slave am I', in which Hamlet contrasts the effectiveness of the Player King's response to an imaginary woe, with his own inability to confront a real evil. This is a curious speech under the circumstances. Short of killing Claudius in cold blood, it is hard to see what else Hamlet could do, and he has a good plan under way to confirm the King's guilt. This suggests that his soliloquy is a rhetorical flourish: not the description of a real delay, but a way of urging himself on to an unpleasant task. Perhaps there is also a hint of self-knowledge here: a recognition that Hamlet, whose fondness for acting is admitted, has been fonder of appearances than he likes to admit. The death of his father under the circumstances confronts him with reality in a brutal form. It is easier to talk about vengeance than to exact it. So it is ironically appropriate that he will use a show or appearance (the play) to put his plan of action into effect. Words will be used to promote deeds. In a play words *are* deeds.

The Act II soliloquy is almost immediately followed by the most famous speech in dramatic literature: 'To be, or not to be . . .', often taken to be a meditation on suicide when linked with I,2,129ff. But such an interpretation goes against the grain of the play and depends upon detaching Hamlet the character from *Hamlet* the play. At this stage of affairs Hamlet has every reason to live: the Ghost has given him new purpose and his vengeance is not complete. It is more likely that Hamlet is reflecting on the comparative merits of leaving things as they are and putting up with them '('To be') or struggling with fate (i.e. Claudius) as the Ghost demands, and suffering the likely consequences ('not to be'). He is, in other words, still stiffening his resolution: this speech leads on from the previous soliloquy.

In the meeting with Ophelia which immediately follows this speech we see that Hamlet's intention to carry on the struggle has won the battle. How much easier to acquiesce in Claudius's victory and marry Ophelia, the woman he loves. Instead, he teases and insults her. This illustrates his resolution, which is dwelt on in the next major speech (III,2,58ff) in the moments before the Dumbshow. In this he praises the man who is not 'passion's slave', and who puts up with good and bad fortune with equal indifference. The speech is addressed to Horatio, but it might equally be addressed as an exhortation to himself. The time for displaying deep feelings is over: what matters now is the rational deliberation on right and justice, irrespective of the consequences mulled over in III,1,56ff. But Hamlet has not quite achieved this admirable state. At the end of II,3 he speaks of drinking hot blood, reminding himself not to be cruel to his mother. His attack on her will be confined to words, not actions.

In view of what is about to happen to Polonius, such a resolution is ironic. Hamlet, having left Claudius alive because he is praying, stabs the arras in his mother's room, expecting to find the King behind it, and kills Polonius instead. He takes the murder more calmly than his mother, so preoccupied is he with persuading his mother to abandon her loyalty to Claudius and participate in her son's plan to convince the king he is really mad. But the plan rebounds. Swallowing the bait, his uncle sends Hamlet off to England, avowedly for his own safety, but really in the company of Rosencrantz and Guildenstern who carry letters which will bring about his death. This is the low point in Hamlet's fortunes. The plan may succeed. Even if it doesn't, he is making enemies, both at court and among the populace. Yet in another soliloquy (IV,4,32ff) he restates and amplifies his determination to seek revenge after his encounter with the troops of Fortinbras, en route to Poland to fight for a scrap of land.

This soliloquy highlights what is, for many modern readers, the contradiction at the heart of the play and the character. On the one hand, Hamlet exalts Man above the beasts because he can fight not merely for survival but for an idea, i.e. honour. On the other hand, the example he gives seems to us shockingly out of proportion with the price to be paid; and the notion of honour is, in any case, contrary to traditional Christian principles, and to general moral sentiment today. Revenge, a central part of the honour code, is not in fashion. There is no way round the conflict, and Hamlet himself has to confront it head-on. For it is only when he understands that revenge is acceptable as the vehicle of impersonal justice and not as the means of violent personal satisfaction that his journey is complete. He has already had a glimmering of this in his words to Horatio (III,1,56ff). In this speech he moves a little closer to it. What he admires about Fortinbras and his men is not the terrible slaughter which their adventure will involve but the fact that they can put their task above their own immediate interests. In resolving to do the same he is approaching the state of mind which can make him say in the last scene of the play 'The readiness is all'.

The audience is edged towards this state of mind by the emotional change involved in Hamlet's absence from the play and his return to the graveyard scene and Ophelia's funeral. The confrontation with Laertes shows that Hamlet's personal pride is still at stake, but this too is conquered in the final scene of the play when he begs for reconciliation with Laertes.

Throughout the play Hamlet is presented to us from different points of view, which deepen our sense of the perspective in which we see his character. We watch him at first hand dealing with the other characters, but he also reveals himself in his soliloquies; and we can approach him through the eyes of the other characters. Each has a different view: Gertrude the doting mother, Claudius the frightened rival, Ophelia the disappointed sweetheart, Polonius the meddling adviser, Horatio the trusted friend, and so on.

More than in any other play by Shakespeare, the spotlight is constantly on one figure, which may do something to explain both his popularity as a character and his enigmatic quality. For though he is presented as sympathetic and passionate, Shakespeare is at no particular pains to make him likeable. On the contrary, he can appear cruel, calculating and cold. But charm is rarely a feature of tragic heroes.

Claudius

Although the play hinges on the struggle between Hamlet and his uncle, the character of Claudius remains comparatively undeveloped. This helps to swing our attention – and our sympathy – towards the hero, but it also threatens to create something of an imbalance within the play. If we are to be impressed by the seriousness of Hamlet's battle with Claudius we have to believe that the King is an interesting and worthy opponent.

Shakespeare makes us believe this in three ways. First, he ensures that while Hamlet does most of the talking, Claudius initiates most of the action. From the murder of the prince's father before the play opens, to the poisoning of the sword at the end, Claudius makes all the running. It is therefore ironically appropriate that, although Hamlet delivers the final blow, the King perishes as a result of his own scheming.

Second, Claudius is shown to be a skilful and wary politician, and a bold plotter, always ready to take advantage of the situation. He kills his sleeping brother in an undetectable way. He marries his sister-in-law. He manipulates Ophelia and Gertrude. He uses Hamlet's murder of Polonius as a way to dispose of the prince; and brilliantly exploits the anger of Laertes to the same end. But all his plans misfire: the Ghost returns to report his own murder, pirates board Hamlet's ship, Gertrude drinks the poison meant for her son, Laertes confesses. But although these eventualities are part of the play's moral scheme – designed to show the inevitable punishment meted out to wickedness – they don't detract from our sense of Claudius's skill and mettle. Above all, they point to a contrast between Claudius's readiness to act and Hamlet's self-declared tardiness.

This contrast is made vividly clear in the scene which most obviously displays Shakespeare's third method of restoring the dramatic balance between the hero and his uncle (the prayer scene, III,3). This is the one moment when Shakespeare gives Claudius the sort of soliloquy otherwise reserved for Hamlet. There are other occasions in the play when the King briefly reveals his private feelings (as opposed to his royal, public self) but never so extensively as here. We are briefly asked to understand and even identify with Claudius's hideous situation, until Hamlet enters with his own disturbing calculations.

Ironically, Claudius finds himself in a complementary predicament to Hamlet. The prince rebukes himself for wondering too much and acting too little. But Claudius, to whom bold action comes easily, cannot find true remorse in his heart: 'My words fly up, my thoughts remain below.'

This soliloquy, like so many of Hamlet's, is a reflection on the nature of action, and might well be compared with the famous lines at III,1,56–88. There, Hamlet discusses the *possible* consequences of 'taking arms'. In his speech, Claudius meditates on the *actual* consequences of evil deeds. Hamlet's entry and his decision not to kill Claudius underlines the parallelism. They both find themselves in the same predicament: they cannot retreat, but they are not sure how to advance. Claudius must deal with the unwelcome but unavoidable effects of his crime, Hamlet must do something about the Ghost's instruction. For a moment, Hamlet's ruthless decision not to kill the King at prayer, lest he dispatch his uncle to Heaven, tilts the balance in Claudius's favour, and the king's final lines after Hamlet's exit have their own tragic tinge.

They also recall the quandary of other Shakespearian kings, especially Macbeth and Henry IV, both of whom seize thrones illegitimately, dispose of their predecessors, and are eventually consumed by guilt and remorse. Shakespeare's interest in monarchy is well known. Explored in the history plays, it here receives another twist. Shakespeare's basic doctrine of government qualifies belief in divine right with the recognition that the maintenance of such right depends to some extent on might, and that a divinely ordained king may be weak or even bad. In *Hamlet*, however, it is made quite clear that Claudius's predecessor was a paragon: strong, brave and just. There is therefore no excuse for removing him. To that extent, Claudius is a far less interesting figure than Henry IV – which is no doubt why the play isn't called *Claudius*, on the analogy with *Henry IV* and *Macbeth*.

And Claudius, despite his great moment in III,3, is neither an admirable nor a virtuous character. In the end virtue is seen to win because Hamlet defeats Claudius not by stratagem or unfair advantage (as would have been the case had he killed him in the prayer scene) but simply by letting things take their course. Claudius brings disaster down on his own head: it is his plot which backfires in the final scene, not Hamlet's plan which succeeds.

Though Hamlet takes his revenge in the end by striking the King down, he is brought to success by default. This is an important consideration in the moral scheme of the play which, as usual in Shakespeare, presents the virtuous as those who knowingly and willingly accept destiny. Claudius, on the other hand, is forever trying to shape matters to his own advantage, and this is his nemesis.

Gertrude

Like Claudius, the character of Gertrude remains comparatively undeveloped. She is Hamlet's mother, Claudius's wife, Old Hamlet's widow, Ophelia's friend, more than she is a figure in her own right. Only briefly, in her great scene with Hamlet (III,4) do we get some sense of her as a person. Usually she is reflecting some aspect of the action, such as Hamlet's reaction to his father's death, or Ophelia's suicide.

We first meet her in I,2 as Claudius's wife and Queen, standing by his side and taking his part against Hamlet. Claudius does most of the talking. To her son's outrage, she joins the King in urging him to cast off what she calls his excessive grief. Her argument – that all men must die – is hardly suited to a recently widowed woman who (if we are to believe Hamlet himself at l.143) doted on her first husband. Depending on the way in which the character is played, we can see her as weak and shallow at this point, or as repressing her deeper feelings in the name of 'getting on with life'. Later in the play, when Hamlet confronts his mother and she reveals her agitation, we may be inclined to favour the second explanation.

Gertrude then disappears from the play until II,2, when she again appears supporting the King, but this time showing rather more concern for her son. Her explanation for his condition – 'I doubt it is no other but the main, His father's death and our o'er-hasty marriage' – is both to the point and more astute than Polonius's over-ingenious ramblings, which she reprimands at l.95.

But Gertrude's first great opportunity comes in the meeting with Hamlet arranged by Polonius (see III,1,184), after the play within the play and Claudius's sterile prayers. By this time the King's guilt is firmly established in the minds of the audience and we are ready to see Hamlet challenge his mother to give up her husband. Yet even in III,4 it is Hamlet who has all the good lines: his mother, like the other characters in the play, reacts to him. There is enough here for a good actress to get hold of, especially when the Ghost enters and Hamlet appears to be talking to himself, but this is a role which Shakespeare only sketches out: everything depends on the way a production balances the two characters.

As a result of the encounter with her son, Gertrude agrees to support his pretence of madness (IV,1,7). Then comes her second great moment: a meeting with the mad Ophelia (IV,5). Here again Gertrude plays second fiddle. Our attention is first on Ophelia, and then on the worried Claudius (IV,5,75ff). But just before Ophelia's entrance, Gertrude makes plain in an aside that she sees how things are going: 'Each toy seems prologue to some great amiss' (l.18).

Ophelia is also the occasion of Gertrude's longest and most touching speech, in which she describes the girl's death (IV,7,165ff) providing a moment of desolate calm amid the bitter plots being hatched by Claudius and Laertes. In the following scene the Queen attends her favourite's burial and reveals her frustrated hopes for the marriage of Ophelia and her son. After this it only remains for her to pledge Hamlet with the poisoned cup and to die – appropriately at her husband's hand. For right up to the end the Queen is an unfortunate bystander – one who, like Rosencrantz and Guildenstern, is caught between the 'pass and fell incensed points/Of mighty opposites'.

Polonius

Polonius is Claudius's chief counsellor, a tragicomic character who brings about his own death by meddling. In this respect he is a pale shadow of his master, Claudius, who brings disaster on himself by refusing to be satisfied with his lot. Polonius, too, can never leave well alone. He is always handing out good advice and cooking up schemes on behalf of his patrons, the King and Queen, whom he bullies because he is quite sure he knows best. They appear to trust him – though with some reservations – and fall in with his schemes.

Although his first appearance as Claudius's adviser and Laertes' father (I,2) is unremarkable, Polonius soon comes into his own at the beginning of Act II, where Shakespeare begins the fun by making him lose track of his own thoughts, so keen is he to domineer over Reynaldo by controlling every aspect of his mission. On a more serious level, Polonius is revealed in this scene as unscrupulous: he is not above ordering his minion to lie if it suits the purpose. Such an outlook may be practical (or 'politic' in the language of the time) but it is also on a par with Claudius's darker misdeeds. Polonius may not know of Old Hamlet's real fate, but he is clearly ready to engage in all sorts of underhand tricks in the name of political necessity. This may not matter in the case of Reynaldo, but it is to have tragic consequences for Ophelia and for himself.

When Ophelia enters as Reynaldo departs, a more sympathetic side of the character emerges: his real feeling for his daughter. But her account of Hamlet's behaviour is also the occasion of an ironic self-estimate when Polonius remarks that older people are inclined to be over-suspicious and over-calculating – two qualities which are to precipitate his own downfall.

In the following scene (II,2) we are introduced to more of Polonius's characteristics: his vanity, his long-windedness, his self-importance. It is worth noting that he already has far more to say for himself than Gertrude, who rebukes his verbosity (II,2,95). Every idea is over-elaborated with similes and qualifications, and his complicated speeches turn out on examination to consist of commonplaces. Though Polonius affects to be clever and subtle, he really has a very ordinary, not to say credulous, mind. Shakespeare parodies in him the character of the politician: the devious schemer who tries to control the lives of others in secret.

Polonius's compliments to himself on his own far-sightedness turn out to be an ironic prelude to fatal mistakes and misunderstandings. Though Hamlet exploits his failings comically in II,2 when he pretends to be mad (171ff) and teases the older man, they take a tragic turn when he kills him in mistake for the King (III,4). This is the direct result of Polonius's passion for spying.

Ophelia

Ophelia is the model of the wronged, innocent maiden: wronged by Hamlet, by Polonius, and by Claudius. She is a pawn in their power struggle, her fate a sign of what happens when things are 'out of joint'.

Like most of Shakespeare's women, Ophelia is no mere ornament or passive victim. Her wit and energy appear in the exchange with Hamlet, and in her firm response to Laertes' lecture (I,3,45ff). Similarly she defends Hamlet in conversation with her father, and rebukes the prince when he oversteps the mark. At the same time, she is the model of the loyal lover, faithful even when there seems little reason to be so. This faithfulness ultimately helps to bring on her madness and death when she is torn between horror at Hamlet's rejection and his murder of her father, and her own innocent devotion.

But just as Gertrude is largely confined to a series of roles, so Ophelia's significance in the play depends on the ways in which Shakespeare uses her to throw light on Hamlet's predicament and the struggle between him and his uncle. We see her first in I,3, being questioned and admonished about her relationship with Hamlet by both Laertes and Polonius. Thus it is this relationship which determines our view of her from the outset. These conversations are also the occasion for both Laertes and his father to enlarge on the general theme of a prince's special rights and obligations, foreshadowing Hamlet's own much later remarks on those who come between 'the pass and fell incensed points/Of mighty opposites' as poor Ophelia does.

In II,1 it is Ophelia who gives the news of Hamlet's 'antic disposition', revealing by the way that she has obeyed her father's instructions (l.108ff). In so doing she is an unconscious agent in her own (and her father's) downfall, for it is this news which prompts Polonius to go to the King, and then to spy on Hamlet in his mother's room.

We only see Hamlet and Ophelia together for the first time in III,1, almost half-way through the play. By this time Hamlet is bitterly rejecting her, though it is not clear how much this is part of his feigned madness, and how much caused by the suspicion that she is being used by Claudius and Polonius. But just as Ophelia proclaimed his madness, so she now speaks a kind of epitaph on his sanity at III,1,152ff. As in I,3, this is made the occasion for a reflection on princely qualities.

Ophelia and Hamlet pursue their verbal duelling during the play scene (III,2), but by the time we next see her (IV,5), Hamlet has killed her father and she is mad, in grim contrast to the prince's feigned lunacy. The mad scene belongs to a well-established tradition, and it provides the opportunity for a bizarre lyrical interlude in which Ophelia mixes scraps of old songs with lamentations and obscene allusions, suggesting that her father's death and her love for Hamlet are inextricably associated in her mind. There is a clear parallel here with Hamlet's mourning for his father and love for his mother. In each case the two emotions are in conflict. In Hamlet this conflict results in melancholy; for Ophelia the outcome is madness. It is this madness, as much as his father's death, which fires Laertes to seek revenge, providing Claudius with a willing tool.

Shortly afterwards Ophelia dies, but she doesn't disappear from the play. Not only is her death the occasion for Gertrude's most beautiful speech at IV,7,165ff, an elegy on the drowned girl: her funeral also provides a spectacular venue for Hamlet and Laertes to confront one another (V,1). But this confrontation, with its aggressive exaggerations, only confirms that Ophelia is little more than an occasion for the acts and feelings of the male characters.

Laertes and Horatio

Laertes and Horatio have complementary roles. Laertes is the epitome of the impetuous, aristocratic young man, who becomes Hamlet's enemy. Horatio is the prince's calm, sceptical, dependable friend. Together with Fortinbras, they make up a trio of contemporaries with whom we are constantly invited to compare Hamlet.

From his first appearance on the stage Laertes provides a foil for the prince, their careers and fates intertwined from the outset. They are both talented and wilful young men, pursuing their studies abroad. But Hamlet is a member of the royal family. Laertes is granted permission to return to Paris, whereas Hamlet is prevented from going back to Wittenberg. Before his departure Laertes warns Ophelia against any entanglement with Hamlet, attributing to the prince some of his own qualities. His heavy-handed advice is comically echoed in Polonius's advice to him.

After this, Laertes disappears from the play until he returns to Denmark to avenge the death of his father, and the comparison with Hamlet becomes even more marked. Unlike that prince, Laertes seems ready to take his revenge without further ado. He bursts into the palace at the head of a mob (IV,5,110) demanding justice, only to encounter there the mad Ophelia. In consequence, he readily falls in with Claudius's plans, adding refinements of his own (IV,7), and even Hamlet's offer of reconciliation (V,2,227ff) does not prevent him from going through with the final duel.

In a play of strong and violent passions, Laertes is a warning against the impetuosity which makes him such a willing tool for Claudius's schemes. It is just this which Hamlet warns himself against when he tells Horatio how much he values the man who is indifferent to Fortune (III,2,59ff). By the time of the duel Hamlet has learnt to accept whatever may befall, while Laertes is still hot for revenge. Horatio is the exact opposite: a cool, sceptical character, praised by Hamlet for just these qualities. As we see from his response to talk of a ghost in Act I, Horatio's first reactions are always cautious. Where Laertes loses his temper, Horatio weighs the possibilities. But his main role is to provide a confidant for Hamlet, allowing some variation on the sequence of soliloquies in which the prince otherwise reveals his inner thoughts.

Minor characters

Four minor characters have important functions in the play. In the first half *Rosencrantz* and *Guildenstern* are used as foils for Hamlet, two of the large company of young men who dominate the play. But they are dull by comparison with the prince. They cannot follow his witty and devious train of thought in II,2, and they believe, like Polonius, that he is mad. In the end, he outwits them by sending the two to their death in his place. This fate is a sign of both the ruthlessness of the times and the price to be paid for guilt by association. Although it does not appear that the two know anything about Claudius's route to power, they are prepared to betray their 'friend' in return for the King's favour, and they show themselves ready to submit to him absolutely (II,2,26–32) just as they dishonestly fawn on Hamlet.

Rosencrantz and Guildenstern are ordinary men who know which side their bread is buttered in dangerous times. Nominally friends of Hamlet, they might normally be pleasant enough companions, but their first loyalty is to the authority in power and they happily work in Claudius's interest. They are not active schemers but willing instruments. As Hamlet himself says 'they did make love to this employment' (V,2,57) and it is therefore appropriate that they are caught up in the struggle between the King and his nephew, who notes in the same speech that

'Tis dangerous when the baser nature comes
Between the pass and fell incensed points
Of mighty opposites.'

At the opposite end of the social scale from the courtiers are the *Grave-digger* and his friend. Like Ophelia's mad scene, the grave-yard is very much a standard part of Jacobean tragedy for obvious reasons: it provides the occasion for gruesome effects, and, more seriously, for meditations on mortality. In this case, Shakespeare also takes the opportunity to introduce the sort of rustic comedy which features in all his tragedies. The characters are not indivi-dualized. The comedy issues largely from their verbal misunder-standings. Like Polonius and Osric, these two are misusers of words. But their parody of courtly verbal jousting and the place in which they talk have the effect of putting the lurid action of the play in perspective: all Claudius's jostling for power and Hamlet's brilliance must, in the end, come to the same thing – death. This is no less powerful for being a truism, because it occurs at the right moment in the play, when Hamlet – and the audience – are ready to accept it.

Osric is a comic version of Polonius, an affected courtier who never uses one word where three will do. Shakespeare was fond of parodying affectation in his comedies, and Osric would fit well among the pedants and fops of *Much Ado About Nothing* or *Love's Labours Lost*. But Osric's character is less important than the moment of his appearance, interrupting the conversation with Horatio in which Hamlet reveals his newly decisive character. Osric's florid phrases and mincing manners contrast vividly with the simplicity of Hamlet's narrative, just as the courtly flummery of the formal duel is a world away from the prince's decision to accept what must come, i.e. his reckoning with Claudius. And Osric stands not only for the triviality and absurdity of court life, but also for its continuity: for him, the duel with Laertes is just another ceremony. Hamlet knows better: once the news from England reaches the court the game will be up. What happens during the next few hours is therefore decisive. The conflict between the King and his nephew is about to be finally resolved.

General questions

1 What is the importance of the Ghost in the play?
Suggested notes for essay answer:

(a) To give information: (I,5) about the murder – Ghost's own words – the knowledge affects the way Claudius is viewed.

(b) To create atmosphere: (I,1+4+5) fear – horror – death; 'this thing', 'dreaded sight'. Talked about before it appears. Link with themes through language:

(1) violence – warlike appearance, armour, martial talk (I,1).
(2) foreboding – evil to state (I,1 Horatio), omen (I,1 Horatio).
(3) disorder – Julius Caesar (I,1 Horatio); 'freeze young blood', 'eyes start from spheres' (I,5 Ghost).
(4) secrecy – silence (I,1 Horatio).

(c) Symbol of goodness – the dead Hamlet embodiment of kingly virtue: 'valiant' (I,1 Horatio), 'goodly king' (I,1 Horatio), 'excellent' (I,2 Hamlet), Hyperion, Jove etc. (III,4 Hamlet).

Dramatic contrast to Claudius: 'revelry' (I,4 Hamlet), Hyperion/satyr (I,2 Hamlet), portraits of both (III,4 Hamlet), goodness corrupted by evil (I,5 blood/poison, polluted milk).

(d) Good/evil uncertainty: 'spirit of health or goblin damned' (I,4 Hamlet).

2 Describe the manner and effect of Hamlet's first appearance.

3 Compare and contrast Laertes and Hamlet.

4 What do Hamlet's soliloquies add to the play?

5 Describe how one of the following images is used in the play: weeds, war, disease, acting, flowers.

6 What happens in Act III, scene 4, and what is its significance in the play?

7 What sort of character is Polonius?

8 Why do women play such a small role in the play?

9 Does Hamlet love Ophelia? If so, why does he behave as he does? If not, what are his feelings for her?

10 Why is Osric in the play?

11 What is revenge tragedy?

12 Identify and describe the different prose styles in the play and comment on their use.

13 Analyse one of Hamlet's soliloquies, commenting on the imagery.

14 What does Ophelia's mad scene contribute to the play?

15 What is Horatio's function in the play?

16 Does Claudius have any good qualities?

17 How much does Gertrude know about the murder of her first husband? Does it matter?

18 Why is the Grave-digger in the play?

19 Explain the significance of the 'play within the play'.

20 Who is Fortinbras and what part does he play?

21 What happens in the prayer scene and why is it significant?

Further reading

The Arden Shakespeare: Hamlet, edited by H. Jenkins (Methuen, 1982)

Shakespeare, A. Burgess (Penguin, 1972)

The Development of Shakespeare's Imagery, W. Clemen (University Paperbacks, 1951)

What Happens in Hamlet, J. D. Wilson (Cambridge University Press, 1951)